"The most valuable books on Christian worship and theology not only provide helpful responses to existing questions but reimagine the questions themselves. In *Deeper Praise*, Dr. Wilson-Bridges offers specific, helpful guidance for those who plan and lead congregational worship and worship music. But, more importantly, she provokes readers to ask deeper questions and find deeper biblical roots to sustain their worship ministry practices."

—NICHOLAS ZORK
DIRECTOR, ANDREWS UNIVERSITY MUSIC & WORSHIP CONFERENCE
MINISTER FOR WORSHIP & THE ARTS,
CHURCH OF THE ADVENT HOPE, NEW YORK CITY

"Dr. Wilson-Bridges issues a clarion call to praise and worship leaders to go deeper in their relationship with God, focusing on His initiative rather than their preferences and tastes. She gently but firmly shakes us out of old covenant thinking and points the way to Holy Ghost-filled praise and worship."

—CEDRIC DENT, PH.D.
MEMBER EMERITUS OF THE 10-TIME
GRAMMY AWARD-WINNING VOCAL GROUP, TAKE 6
PROFESSOR OF MUSIC, MIDDLE TENNESSEE STATE UNIVERSITY

"Dr. Wilson-Bridges' book provides us with "deep" spiritual insight on what authentic praise and worship is. The principles shared are timeless and transformational. This is a must read for every worship leader AND believer desiring an intimate and uncompromised relationship with God, regardless of their denomination or cultural background."

—DR. SANDRA UPTON
VICE PRESIDENT, EDUCATIONAL INITIATIVES
CULTURAL INTELLIGENCE CENTER LLC, HOLT MICHIGAN

"This book is a must for any individual in ministry, as well as for any church serious about worship. We live in a society where so much of what we do is based on how we "feel". And if it "feels" good, then it must be. Church worship has been modified to make people feel good, and therefore attract more worshipers. But worship is more than that. Worship is what we offer (bring) to the Lord. Understanding true worship unlocks a deeper walk, and therefore relationship, with God. In this very powerful book, Dr. Cheryl Wilson-Bridges demonstrates, from a complete Biblical perspective, what are the components (modes) of praise, how to prepare (individually and corporately) for worship, and when the components of worship fit into the perfect place to create a worship experience that brings us as close to our Heavenly Father as possible. If you are serious about worship, please read this book. It can transform your personal worship, and the worship of your church!"

—JAIME JORGE
RECORDING ARTIST, AUTHOR,
MOTIVATIONAL/INSPIRATIONAL SPEAKER

"In *Deeper Praise*, once again Dr. Wilson-Bridges demonstrates that she understands the 'big' picture when it comes to the somewhat confusing and controversial topic of worship. The message that leaps from each page is that worship goes much deeper than style, preference or the latest ecclesiastical fad, but it is walking in complete obedience with the Savior. I highly recommend *Deeper Praise* to anyone who desires a deeper understanding of the role worship is to have in our daily lives as well as in the life of the church."

—CHARLES A. TAPP
SENIOR PASTOR, SLIGO SEVENTH-DAY ADVENTIST CHURCH,
TAKOMA PARK, MARYLAND

Deeper
PRAISE

DR. CHERYL WILSON-BRIDGES

CREATION
HOUSE

Back cover photo: Ludmila Leito, All Shades of Gray Photography
Back cover photo hair and makeup: Sharon Nichols-Linkins and
Stephanie Bell

Library of Congress Control Number: 2015913998
International Standard Book Number: 978-1-62998-496-4
E-book International Standard Book Number: 978-1-62998-497-1

While the author has made every effort to provide accurate telephone
numbers and Internet addresses at the time of publication, neither the
publisher nor the author assumes any responsibility for errors or for
changes that occur after publication.

First edition

16 17 18 19 20 — 987654321
Printed in Canada

To:

The Levites

To those who never want to thirst again
in praise and worship, drink deep from
the ocean of God's Holy Word.

Conrad and Darius
Thank you for the deepest love, support, and faith
that any wife and mother could ever imagine.

Pastor Henry M. Wright and the
Community Praise Center Church Family
Thank you for taking me *deeper*.
(1995–2013)

TABLE OF CONTENTS

Part I:
Return

Part II:
Reveal

FOREWORD

*D*EEPER PRAISE IS exactly that! One will never know the depths of worship by playing it safe in the shallows. You know the shallows—where your feet are still firmly planted on the sand...where you can resist the pull of the undertow...where you are still in control. In order to go deeper, one must launch out away from the safety of the shoreline, where your feet no longer touch the ground and you must surrender to the current. God's current will rarely go where your flesh wants to go. God's current, if yielded to, will take you to a place in worship that will change your heart and life forever. And once you have been to that place, you will never settle for anything less.

That place is the place of God's presence—His overwhelming and all-consuming presence where words fail us and we find ourselves on our faces undone. *Deeper Praise* is all about a holy summons to that place where we all want to be: that place where we slip from the natural into the supernatural; that place where we are at peace; that place where we realize who we really are and who we are meant to be. My dear friend Cheryl is calling us all to this place and lets us know that it is only accessible through deeper praise.

This book does not mince words; we have no time for that. It cuts to the heart of the severity of our situation in the church today. Many worship a God they have no day-to-day relationship with. Others use the platform they have been given like a stage, while still others worship a god of their own making rather than the God of Abraham, Isaac, and Jacob. We go from one extreme to another—from anything goes to not allowing anything new to take place. Some pastors and worship leaders try to manipulate and cajole congregations into certain aspects of worship without realizing that you can never make someone worship. While we bark and bicker about style and liturgics, the lost of this world still need to be loved into the arms of God.

Allow me to illustrate my point further. Not long ago I served at a church where the senior pastor asked me, "How do you think the worship services are going?" This is a question that I answered frequently, and my answers were never well received. So after ignoring my answers for several years, one day he said, "We are going to poll the congregation and see what they'd like to do in our worship services. That will tell us what we should do."

This is where we find ourselves in many places in the church today. Rather than asking God what His heart would desire in worship and what would please Him, we'd rather poll the people—see which way the wind is blowing today; set up a worship committee to study it all; and pass out a questionnaire to see if people liked the music or not, etc.,—all the while the heart of the Lord grieves.

Cheryl starts this book off with a powerful verse from the life of Israel where Moses finally puts his foot down and says, "Whoever is on the Lord's side—come to me!" And all the sons of Levi (the worship leaders) gathered themselves to him (see Exod. 32:26). After thousands of years, the Holy Spirit is still asking, "Who *is* on the Lord's side?" This beautiful book lets you know right up front that if you are to be on the Lord's side it will require humility, a teachable spirit, and brokenness—things God can use. God cannot use us if we are full of pride, addicted to the sin of preference, and critical of others' worship.

Deeper Praise calls us to hone our craft and calling by reminding us that this is only possible if we are led by the Holy Spirit. We can have all the talent in the world, but if the touch of God (the anointing) is not on our life and our song, it will never change a person. If we are not taking in, what do we have to give out? So into the deep we go, yielding to the current that will take us to where we are called and purposed to be: that place in God where we are no longer in control, but where we are sensitive to the touch and whisper of His Spirit's voice who calls us to deeper praise!

—DAVID M. EDWARDS
Songwriter, Artist, Author, Educator
Artist-in-Residence, International Center for Worship,
Regent University

PREFACE

*I*N MARCH 2012, Oscar-winning filmmaker and National Geographic Explorer-in-Residence James Cameron emerged from his successful solo dive to the Mariana Trench, the deepest part of the ocean. His expedition entailed a dive that submerged him seven miles beneath the Pacific Ocean which is deeper than Mount Everest is high. Although Cameron, maker of blockbuster, mega-hit movies like *The Titanic* and *Avatar,* has undoubtedly reached the pinnacle of Hollywood success, something in his soul compelled him to go deeper. Cameron has an unquenchable thirst to explore beyond the visible, to reach the unreachable, to be immersed and plunge into the deep, dark, oceanic depths beyond human comprehension. The human quest to go deeper is mystifying.

Yet in today's modern society of relativity and no absolutes, not everyone desires to go *deeper.* For most people, deeper is uncomfortable and frightening. For most people, deeper is a socially unacceptable and time-consuming notion. We live in a secular society that embraces a blatant disregard for absolute truth and lauds shallowness and immediate gratification. So why persistently search for the unknown? We search for the unknown because deep down inside we truly believe there is always something more to gain or to give. So what about us as Christians who live in this modern society? Why are we to search deeper? What should we gain or give?

The Bible relentlessly illustrates that God's people must have a deep relationship with Him. In Daniel 2:22, after God revealed Nebuchadnezzar's dream, the prophet Daniel exclaimed, "He reveals deep and hidden things; he knows what lies in darkness, and light dwells with him" (NIV). In Psalm 42:7, the master musician King David cries out in his desperate yearning for God, "Deep calls unto deep at the noise of Your waterfalls; all Your waves and billows have gone over me" (NKJV). Now I must admit, this sounds more like drowning than a deep praise experience. Yet despite his trials, David understood that to be a *true worshiper*, you first have to be completely submerged in the Spirit of God to experience the waves of His overflowing grace. Only then will you fully surrender to the tide of God's love and allow the Holy Spirit to wash over you. Only then will you *truly* give praise.

So why is it that so many of us musicians who lead church worship do not delve into the deep, unknown ocean of God's Holy Word or bathe in the pouring waterfall of His Holy Spirit? Instead we remain safely on the sunny shores, beached and playing in the shifting sands of artistry, culture, and personal preference. Our church worship has become dry, wide, and loose just like the sands of the seashore. We have no need for biblical structure; our praise is not drenched in the Word of God; and we seem to desire only the fulfillment shallowly gleaned from mood-shaping music or the artistic fads of the day. In its dryness, our musical praise has become spirited yet shallow, liturgical but not long lasting, full of artistry but not ministry, musical but not missional. Nevertheless, deep inside our hearts we thirst for the ever-flowing waters of pure praise that would transform us and create a sea of worshipers.

The music of the church is foundational to its existence. Jesus sang a hymn with His disciples after eating the Last Supper (see Mark 14:26). In a Bible study guide entitled *Worship*, author Rosalie Zinke admits, "There is no question that music and praise are part of our worship experience. Music has the power to touch us and move us that other forms of communication do not seem to have. At its purest and finest, music seems to lift us into the very presence of the Lord."[1] So if music lifts us into the majestic presence of the Lord, then why is there so much controversy with regard to church music? Can there be contention and chaos in the presence of the Lord? Can the Master produce mayhem?

Absolutely not! God is not the author of confusion (see 1 Cor. 14:33). So I ask you then, "What is the real problem with our music and praise?" Okay, before you answer the question, let me share with you my beliefs. I believe we have a serious problem with our motives and methods for giving musical praise. This dilemma is so pervasive and widely accepted in the church today that we no longer realize there is an insidious issue. We have accepted the shifting sands of worship and are now building sandcastles that cannot withstand the winds of strife. I believe we have lost our curiosity to be spiritual explorers searching for the deeper things of God. We are content with our permissive praise, while God longs for our hearts and minds to be filled with His purposeful praise. I believe we have put music above the Master, sadly letting dysfunctional practices seep into our pews and pervert our songs.

I believe our problem is that the musical praise we offer should be filled with God's majesty, but instead it is a tragedy often cited as the culprit for the mayhem in our churches. Our problem is that we blame the style, when the music is not worshipful or disruptive, yet we do not search God's Word for practical solutions. A mess instead of a message is widespread when our motives and methods are self-soothing or self-centered instead of God-seeking. The problem is the lack of pastoral leadership in musical praise and worship, when the Bible clearly outlines a comprehensive priestly leadership model for music ministry. I believe we find ourselves in a predicament when we are diligent to adore the melodies and the musicians, but not the God who created us and music for His delight. Our praise is parched because we sit on sandy shores sunbathing, peering at the ocean with little or no desire to dive in deep. Now I ask you again, "What do you believe is the real problem with our music and praise?"

The purpose of this book, *Deeper Praise: Music, Majesty, or Mayhem,* is to provide you with biblical principles to guide your selection of music and genuine praise practices that truly please God. *Deeper Praise* gives a personal, practical, and biblical account of numerous worshipers both past and present who have committed their lives to the unfathomable quest to offer praise that glorifies God *alone*. The practical tips and scriptural principles revealed in this book will transform your society, community, church, family, and life! I have written this book as a praise and worship guide for you to use at home and in church. I am offering you this book because I am convinced that it is our lack of biblical knowledge, spiritual leadership, and practical application that creates the confusion which allows us to offer God institutionalized, preferential praise instead of intentional, purposeful praise. If we surrender and freely give God deeper praise, we will experience the wondrous, matchless presence of His glory, majesty, and power.

There are so many people that I would like to thank who have helped me in the writing of this book. The number of people who have contributed to my ideas, principles, research, and concepts are immeasurable. However, I would like to mention just a few by name. I would like to acknowledge my husband, Conrad, and son, Darius, who have been with me all the way on my pastoral journey. They have listened patiently to all my numerous ideas, concepts, drafts, trials, and triumphs with wisdom, patience, kindness, love, jokes, and compassion. I would like to thank my parents, Norris and Virginia Wilson, who always believe in me, no matter how inconceivable my latest idea sounds.

I would like to thank my siblings, Hubert (deceased), Donmarie, Noralyn (deceased), and Eric for always being there for me. I would like to thank each one of them for teaching me that no challenge is too great for us to overcome as a family. They taught me that love sprinkled with determination can conquer all, and I continue to discover that our family bond will never be broken— not even by death.

I would like to thank my former senior pastor Henry M. Wright, who was the Senior Pastor of the Community Praise Center (CPC)

Seventh-day Adventist church during my tenure as the Minister of Music from 2000 to 2013. I would like to thank the CPC pastoral staff, the music and worship ministry teams, and the CPC church family who were more than supportive and worked alongside me to use the worship services as a "living lab" to engage God in deeper praise. I would like to thank my present senior pastor Charles A. Tapp, who is the Senior Pastor of the Sligo Seventh-day Adventist church. He has been a great leader, friend, mentor, and wise counselor to me all throughout this process. I will be forever grateful. I would like to thank our Sligo pastoral team, Don McFarlane, Gerry Lopez, Pranitha Fielder, Richard Castillo, Joseph Khabbaz, and our office staff. These pastors and colleagues have been the best and most supportive ministry team ever. I could not have done this without your prayers, support, and camaraderie. Finally, I would like to thank my Sligo Church family. Your diversity, compassion, love of ministry, and dedication to God inspires me. I look forward to designing worship with you that exceeds our dreams and brings God glorious praise.

Special thanks to my Levite Praise Ministry team (Michelle Riley-Jones, Regina Reaves, Dave Cavins, Earlgarth Greaves, Loren Mulraine, Esq., and Leslie Bridges); each one of you has supported God's plan for me to be a vessel through which He makes a sea of worshipers. I want to thank each one of the musicians, singers, artists, worshipers, friends, and Levites that I have met when I travel to present seminars, preach sermons, teach classes, participate in concerts, present conferences, take part in panel discussions, or just attend worship services. Each one of you has enriched my life with your questions, comments, suggestions, support, encouragements, late-night discussions, long, provocative emails, Skype calls, and much, much more. All of your input has been food for this book and my soul.

Finally I want to thank you, the reader, for your support and commitment to dive into the waters of worship on a pioneering voyage to discover a deeper understanding of praise and music in the church. I pray you enjoy the journey.

Like the bottom of the sea, praise to God is a mystery. But when our praise runs deep, it lifts us high to the courts of heaven where angels tread and bow their heads to the Lord of hosts. Jesus Christ, our heavenly High Priest leads us in worship to the Father, and we receive power to boldly go and spread the Gospel message to all the world. This is the why *Deeper Praise* is essential! Like the bottom of the ocean, praise is endless, mysterious, rich, abounding with new life, beauty, and God's majesty. But without the courage and determination to jump in as spiritual explorers to deeper praise, we are left on the shores of self-satisfaction wondering why our faith is so feeble.

Ephesians 3:17–19 reads, "That Christ may dwell in your hearts through faith; that you, being rooted and grounded in love, may be able to comprehend with all the saints what is the width and length and depth and height—to know the love of Christ that passes knowledge; that you may be filled with all the fullness of God." I pray that this book *Deeper Praise* will start you on a voyage to seek God with an unquenchable thirst for His loving presence, so you can praise Him eternally with your whole heart.

ENDNOTE

1.   Rosalie Zinke, *Worship* (Nampa, ID: Pacific Press, 2011), 50.

INTRODUCTION

"*T*HAT'S DEEP." I hear this saying used frequently in our modern culture to express something that we consider profound, heartfelt, great, intense, heavy, penetrating, mysterious, or far below the surface. We use this lingo often to show our appreciation, admiration, or affirmation for extensive knowledge or understanding of a concept or practice. We use another phrase—"in deep"—to suggest that we are inextricably connected to something or may even have gone too far into a situation. For our culture today, the word *deep* implies an endless plunge that leaves you immersed and covered.

Yet when it comes to giving God praise, I hear different language. The colloquialism frequently used by many of our worship leaders today is "*I'm here to get my praise on.*" I have discovered this saying does not lead us to be God-focused, nor does it challenge us to go deep in praise. The first part of the phrase "I'm here" says that *I have arrived.* I am here, so now the focus is on me. The words "get my" suggests that praise is something for me. It is something that I myself can receive or attain. This saying signifies that praise is for *my* possession, *my* use, and *my* enjoyment. Praise is *mine* to get and to give. Then, once I *get my praise*, I put *my praise on*—which further hints that my praise is not deep but *remains on the surface.* My praise is placed on top of the object I adore to be applied or removed at *my will.* For many Christians, this shallow expression, "I'm here to get my praise on" has a deeper meaning. It is more than just church jargon. It has become church life!

So often in our church worship what we put on is a "praise show."

We have our worship lights, cameras, and the stage we call our pulpit is set for action. Then on cue, the band counts us in, and we respond to the music for our praise show to begin. We convince ourselves that we are offering God authentic praise because good or even great music is being sung and played. But if you don't have the right motives and methods, you can offer what seems like worship to you, yet sadly God will not be pleased with your praise. Your worship is not focused on the King of kings but on the fleeting emotions that the music brings.

> Your praise music can be played with excellence, yet if it is out of godly order, the only one being played is *you*.

When the Israelites felt they had no leader because Moses was on Mount Sinai with God, they longed for the comforts of Egypt. Succumbing to their fear, they lacked faith. So they clamored for the heathen Egyptian worship that had become strangely familiar. At Aaron's request, they volunteered their precious belongings so he could create a golden calf. Then they began the show. They began to "play worship." In Exodus 32:5–6, the Bible describes the chaotic scene: "So when Aaron saw it, he built an altar before it. And Aaron made a proclamation and said, 'Tomorrow is a feast to the LORD.' Then they rose early on the next day, offered burnt offerings, and brought peace offerings; and the people sat down to eat and drink, and rose up to *play*."

Today we are just like the Israelites playing worship in the sands of the Sinai desert. We too have given away our precious belongings—our youth and talented musicians—to create the god of our choosing, a golden calf called praise music.

We stand in the sandy desert near to God, but we are not seeking His presence. Then our religious revelry begins as we praise and worship. Just like the Israelites, without God-centered worship and spiritual leadership, we find ourselves looking back at Egypt. Instead of deeper praise to please God, we decide to appease each other. Rather than pure praise, our perverted practices have led us in deep. Our worship is no longer covered by the blood of Jesus Christ and watered by God's Holy Word; instead, it is soaked in creeping compromise. Because of this unholy mixture, we find ourselves sinking, maybe even drowning in spiritual quicksand. Our praise is no longer rooted in God's Word but anchored by our longing for Egypt filled with its pagan traditions, culture, style, and rituals.

It is time for us to return to
our Red Sea Experience!

You see, to get to the Red Sea, the Israelites had to be led by God across the arid desert and travel in the wilderness. Millions of people maintained orderly ranks (Exod. 13:18), even as they fled from the Egyptian pharaoh, ruler of the most powerful army in the world. No matter what your problem, there is always room for structure and order among God's people. But when they arrived at the massive Red Sea with the Egyptian army pursuing them and desert all around, they pushed through their fear and held on to their faith. They obeyed Moses' order to "stand still, and see the salvation of the Lord" (Exod. 14:13). Are we standing still in worship, waiting for the salvation of the LORD? Or have we set up our camps in the wilderness where we allow our fear of the Egyptians with their heathen beliefs to dictate our worship practice?

To get to the Promised Land, the Israelites had to walk on the dry ground at the bottom of the sea with walls of water all around them. They had to be led by God to the deepest point—the depths of the Red Sea—to find salvation. In their quest for God, they had to travel far below the surface to find their true faith and be delivered from the dangers of assimilating to Egyptian worship culture. Now is the time for us to be like the Israelites at the Red Sea! We can no longer be slaves to the music, tradition, culture, personal preferences, rigid rituals, or praise and worship fads of our day. It is time for us to come out of Egypt and go deeper in God's Word. When we are led to God's Word by our Savior Jesus Christ, each scripture will form a wall of protection and guidance around our praise practices. We must surrender our will to God and become relentless spiritual explorers searching for the truth of God's Word in musical praise.

Just the mere fact that you have purchased this book makes you a worship seeker. So, my friend and fellow Levite, here is how I suggest that you begin your deep praise exploration. This book, *Deeper Praise: Music, Majesty, or Mayhem,* has two vital parts that should be read in consecutive order. In the first part, "Return," you will discover that chapter 1 expounds on the "Faith of Our Fathers" and will show you how to return to the praise practices of the patriarchs through a review of the Old Testament Levites. We will examine the Levites' commitment to offer God true praise despite enormous peer pressure, and we will learn vital lessons from their distinct call to the priesthood and worship leadership. In chapter 2, "Total Praise," we will look at the psalmist David who showed us that we need more than mere musical talent to give God total praise. We will also identify, unpack, and apply God's list of seven spiritual characteristics for the sanctuary artist, along with techniques for pastoring members with musical praise. Lastly, we will define biblical praise and then look at the seven modes of praise that God prescribes to give Him glory. In chapter 3, "Ordinary People," we will continue to study David's life and see how he dealt with faith versus fame. We will also discover that although God uses ordinary people, being an artist for God is no ordinary task. Then we will deepen our praise practices by an investigation into the mystery of Uzzah's death and see how David's failed and successful worship attempts apply to us today. In chapter 4, "Running Back to You," we will examine the Book of Psalms as God's holy hymnal that can be used as a handbook for today's praise music. We will identify timeless principles for the structure of musical praise and apply them to styles such as Gospel, Contemporary Christian, and Classical music, etc., to understand how various genres can be offered to God in pleasing praise.

In the second part, "Reveal," we will get a clear view of biblical praise principles. In chapter 5, "Into My Heart," you will learn practical and proven techniques as we evaluate the model of the ancient Israelite sanctuary and apply it purposefully to our worship services. Then we will launch a Holy Spirit analysis of musical styles to uncover what type of heartfelt praise music is acceptable for the sanctuary. In chapter 6, "I Surrender All," you will be enlightened about the process of submission and sincere surrender in worship. We will look at the early experiences in the ministry of Jesus Christ to help you grasp how to refresh and deepen your personal praise relationship with God. We will also redefine the role of the worship leader by understanding Jesus' call to ministry and discipleship. In chapter 7, "In Christ Alone," we will continue to examine the ministry of Jesus Christ and center on the Last Supper and His crucifixion. We will review techniques and worship practices that define missional praise. We will outline methods for Christ-centered praise and provide practical steps to keep our praise music focused on Jesus. Then we will delve into cultural praise and see how Christ interacted with different cultures. Finally, we will view Christian culture through the lens of the Cross. Each chapter will be complete with Levite Lessons and Practical Praise Questions that include constructive methods to employ the principles you have learned.

In her book *Testimonies for the Church,* author Ellen White tells us that "to the humble believing soul, the house of God on earth is the gate of heaven. The song of praise, the prayer, the words spoken by Christ's representatives, are God's appointed agencies to prepare a people for the church above, for that loftier worship into which there can enter nothing that defileth."[1] I pray that this book, *Deeper Praise,* will take you on an indescribable praise expedition that will wash you from the musical shores of self-gratification and cast you into the deep cleansing waves of God's praise presence, power, and love.

ENDNOTE

1.   Ellen G. White, *Testimonies for the Church, vol. 5* (Mountain View, CA: Pacific Press, 1948), 491.

PART I:

Return

Chapter 1

FAITH OF OUR FATHERS

Then Moses stood in the entrance of the camp, and said,
"Whoever is on the LORD's side—come to me!" And all
the sons of Levi gathered themselves together to him.

—EXODUS 32:26

HIGH PRAISE

A CAPTIVATING YET STRANGE song filled the air. Its haunting melody and ringing harmonies rose high to the majestic summit of Mount Sinai. This peculiar song hovered in the clean, crisp air until it slowly ascended to the consecrated cloud and caught the attention of the mountain's occupants. There were three spectators on the holy mountain that day: Joshua, Moses, and God. The sound of sacrilegious singing swirled around the rugged peaks and quickly began to shift the mountain's sacred atmosphere. The Israelites in the valley below were engaged in idol worship. Shockingly, instead of worshiping the living God on the mountain, they were in the valley shamelessly singing praise to a golden calf molded by Aaron at their request.

Only three months after God's miraculous display of His deliverance power at the Red Sea, the Israelites abandoned their faith. They were no longer slaves to the Egyptian pharaohs, yet in the desert they remained shackled by fantasies of their heathen past. In haste, instead of glorifying God, they decided to return to an Egyptian style of worship. Aaron and the Israelite leaders should have known better. To reassure the people of God's providence in the Sinai valley, Aaron should have ushered in a posture of pure praise. He could have recreated the atmosphere of adoration and jubilation sung in the melodies of Moses and Miriam once safely across the Red Sea (Exod. 15). But instead, the people's doubt in Moses' return from the mountain as well as Aaron's lack of leadership placed the Israelites in a spiritual drought that allowed fear and folly to seal their fate. They attempted to offer praise to God in a manner that was sorely displeasing to Him. Therefore their worship was worthless. In exalting the golden calf, the worship of the Lord had been blended with the symbols of Baal and other fertility gods. Their worship to God was now fused with falsehood. This unholy mingling caused musical mayhem.

As the sounds of musical mayhem made its way up high to the mountain's peak, each observer—Joshua, Moses, and God—shared different opinions of the revelry below. Just like our praise and worship music today, we each have different opinions on what is appropriate. We listen to the same songs yet come away with widely different views on the sacredness or sinfulness of the music. Similarly, on Mount Sinai, each onlooker judged separately while listening to the same praise song.

Joshua, the youngest and least spiritually mature, was perched on a nearby peak below Moses and God. From his spiritual vantage point, Joshua only heard noise (Exod. 32:17). He assessed the situation and determined that the camp was being threatened; he concluded the sound was the noise of war. The Hebrew word for noise, *qowl,* is defined as "the voice or the sound of an instrument used in *lightness* or *frivolity.*"[1]

The sound of singing that Joshua heard lacked seriousness. It was self-indulgent and carefree. It was of little weight, worth, or importance. It was not deep! Joshua heard a song without spiritual purpose. It was a song that announced strife and contention. So it is no wonder that Joshua surmised that this song was a war song. Yet the war song Joshua heard did not signify fighting such as hand-to-hand combat. In God's presence, Joshua heard a song that signaled a war within.

Moses was on the mountain, covered in the cloud of God's presence. As a former prince of Egypt, Moses knew the unsettling behaviors of the Israelites well. He was accustomed to hearing about their numerous rebellions, complaints, and raucous activities that had to be staid by the overseer's whip. In Egypt, he defended the Israelites by risking his own life and royal reputation. However, as a fugitive in Midian, Moses spent quiet, meditative time with God. During this serene reprieve, God called Moses and revealed His plan of deliverance for His people. Now after forty years of spiritual growth, Moses was God's friend (Exod. 33:11). Therefore, having deep spiritual discernment, Moses was quickly able to identify the mayhem he heard in the Israelite camp.

I can assure you that in the mayhem that becomes misguided praise music, you will always see division and experience a feeling of separation. In this musical mayhem, opposing sides will form among your friends, in your home, and in your church. These contentious divisions will be painfully clear to you. However, what will remain unclear without deep spiritual maturity is which side is the right side—in other words, which side is God's side.

Moses identified these two sides in his masterful response to Joshua. Exodus 32:18 reads, "He said, 'It is not the noise of the shout of victory, nor the noise of the cry of defeat, but the sound of singing I hear.'"

The Hebrew word that Moses used for singing, `anah, is defined as "to be occupied or busy with, to afflict, oppress, humble, weaken oneself, become low and humiliate."[2] Moses knew that this form of singing was not due to the horrors of war or the people's desire to be holy; it was a self-imposed overindulgence that would lead to division, certain humiliation, and spiritual weakness. Sin results in separation from God (Gen. 3:23–24). In the valley below, the Israelites were busy. They were occupied with their songs, yet their music was in no way worship to God. The Israelites' frenzied singing was sinful because they dared to offer worship to Almighty God with an idol, a golden calf, which for the Egyptians signified the bull god, an embodiment of Baal. In their unholy revelry, they had become oppressed and spiritually weakened. They had separated themselves from the Most High God and chosen the side of an idol. Their need for expediency, personal preference, and self-gratification made them choose a substitute for God that would bring them to the lowest depths of depravity.

Today, the noise of war and divisiveness is being waged in our church pews. Maybe you have experienced this divisive phenomenon in your own church. As I travel the globe, I see church members bicker, fight, and ultimately choose sides to promote their rigid, personal opinions on praise and worship with little to no comprehensive biblical foundation. Without Scripture to guide and formulate our opinions, we worship in vain. Unknowingly, we choose the wrong side as we sing our songs in the camp of preference and self-centeredness. Then, with all our might, we play and offer our worship to an idol—praise music—that has slowly and secretly become our golden calf.

Without biblical direction, we select the winners and losers based on the most acceptable praise genre of the masses. In our efforts to win the worship wars, some of us choose the side of classical music, the hymns, or anthems of the church. Others choose the side of gospel, spirituals, or contemporary Christian music (CCM). We exile those who choose genres like jazz, rap, Christian rock, or pop music based solely on personal preference, historical research, or the rapidly changing waves of musical fads. In this unstable state, the winning and losing sides alternate erratically. In such a volatile environment, the winning and losing camps tend to easily reach their boiling points. People's opinions on the appropriateness of the worship music continue to ebb and flow. Yet in this mayhem, the undercurrents of frustration and contention continue to flood our pews.

While we may have noble intentions, we fiercely fight the worship wars and base our view of victory on personal preference. Still we never stop to notice that Jesus Christ is not fighting our battle, nor is God pleased with our praise. In true praise, there are no two sides and no competition. In true praise, there are no winners and no losers. In true praise, there is only one side united as one body, with one holy purpose. In true praise, we unite our sacred songs of praise to worship the One True God—our Lord Savior Jesus Christ.

On the sacred mountain, the sovereign God saw the people's perversion, and then informed Moses of the chaos in the valley. Exodus 32:7–8, 10 (NIV) reads,

> Then the LORD said to Moses, "Go down, because your people, whom you brought up out of Egypt, have become corrupt. They have been quick to turn away from what I have commanded them and have made themselves an idol cast in the shape of a calf. They have bowed down to it and sacrificed to it and have said, 'These are your gods, Israel, who brought you up out of Egypt.'....Now leave me alone so that my anger may burn against them and I may destroy them. Then I will make you into a great nation."

The Hebrew word that God used for corrupt is *shachath,* which means "to destroy, ruin, decay, pervert."[3] It is also used to describe the ruin of humankind that provoked the flood (Gen. 6:12). In this moment, God knew that the Israelites' hearts had become utterly corrupted and only a flood of His judgment could wash away their sins. But Moses pleaded with the Lord on Israel's behalf. He begged God to have mercy and to keep His promises of blessing and prosperity to their forefathers.

Can you imagine how God must have felt? The Israelites' rebellion made God so angry that He threatened to destroy His beloved people! It was because of His deep, everlasting love that God had just delivered Israel from certain death and destruction. In Egypt, He performed astounding miracles to deliver Israel to prove His unconditional love and protection. Then God led the Israelites safely through the Red Sea to Mount Sinai so He could shower His love on them in an intimate, secluded setting. God wanted to meet His beloved Israel face to face. He longed for them to return to the affectionate relationship in the Garden of Eden that allowed mankind to experience His glorious presence (Gen. 3:8). So at Sinai, God invited His chosen people into His holy presence so they could feel the depths of His love. Yet after a pledge of commitment (Exod. 24:3), within just a few days they had broken their promise to serve God only.

Even in our rebellion and complete rejection, God's feelings toward us never change. God is merciful and loves us with an everlasting love despite our sinful condition. So God listened to Moses' plea to save Israel and began a process that would eradicate four hundred years of mental, physical, and spiritual slavery. The Israelites had been corrupted by fear, pride, and personal preference (the god of their own choosing), and they rushed to resolve their problems without godly direction. Now the Israelites had rejected God by their sinful methods and selfish motives expressed in their idol worship. Yet lovingly, God still enacted His plan to separate Israel from the heathen Egyptians and ordain them as a holy nation.

When your praise becomes self-centered and self-gratifying, first you experience a war within. You ask yourself questions like "Why can't I play or sing the music *I feel* is worshipful?" "Why should I listen to anyone else about how *I should* praise?" Then once you succumb to Satan's sly temptations, your arrogance and pride will separate you from your desire to be in God's presence. At first you may not be aware of the division in your soul. But signs of this worship turmoil can be seen in your disposition. You become unbearable, intolerable, and self-righteous. Negative feelings of discontent and disdain for those who worship in a way that does not meet your standards begins to abound and infect your heart and mind.

Then you will begin to fight and quarrel with anyone who opposes your viewpoint. You may even feel compelled to separate yourself from anyone who does not share your opinions. Your praise becomes frenzied and based solely on religious ritual, not spiritual sincerity. Instead of being a *praise warrior* fighting for the cause of Christ, you become a *praise worrier* wreaking havoc and discord under the guise of defending God's praise. But God does not need our defense. On the contrary, He longs for our surrender so that in our offering of genuine worship He can saturate us with His love.

What a chaotic mess! What a terrifying scene that must have been when Moses angrily came pelting down the mountain with the Ten Commandments, crashing the stone tablets into pieces! This angry display signified that God's covenant had also been broken. As he descended the slope, Moses recounted the miracles God performed at the Red Sea. He remembered that the Egyptians were on one side of the shore while the Israelites stood safely on the opposite side. There is a divide that is necessary in authentic worship, but it is not among God's people. In true worship, a divine divide is experienced. In true worship, you will sense the divinely imposed separation between light and darkness, good and evil, God's standards and Satan's seductions, followers of Jesus Christ and enemies of God's commands. You will sense spiritual warfare.

The sight of the people's idolatry, along with Aaron's pitiful excuses to blame the multitude, Moses' lengthy departure, and even the molten calf for his failings riled up Moses even more! Yet this time instead of anger, Moses became emboldened by God's Spirit. He saw that the people were wild. They chose to do whatever seemed right to them and not what God had commanded (Deut. 12:8). This dangerous stance against God's commands could only breed outright rebellion. Then Moses stood in the entrance of the camp and made a clarion call. He said, "Whoever is on the LORD's side—come to me!" (Exod. 32:25–26). And all the sons of Levi came to him!

The Bible mentions no other persons or Israelite tribes that came to Moses that day. Moses gave everyone the opportunity to repent and return to God. But only the Levites responded. Only one tribe, the Levites, from all twelve of the Israelite tribes, came when Moses made a call asking the people to choose worship on God's side. The Levites alone were united by their ardent belief in God, and they knew the sounds of pure praise. Out of all the Israelite tribes, only the Levites recognized that the singing in the camp that day was sinful. Only the Levites knew the sound of singing that would reverence God and offer authentic praise.

LEVITE PRAISE

Why was it that the Levites were the only Israelite tribe who knew the difference between true praise singing and idol worship? Honestly, I don't know. The Bible does not make it crystal clear why the Levites alone were able to separate themselves from the other eleven tribes and commit to true worship. How were they able to remain pure and refrain from idolatry when everyone else in the crowd was doing it? How did they resist such enormous peer pressure? At this point, not all the Levites were called to be priests. This honor had only been given to Aaron and his sons (Exod. 29:9). Yet the Bible does tell us that when Levi was born to his parents Jacob and Leah, his name meant "attached to me" (Gen. 29:34). Leah hoped this third son would improve her troubled relationship with her unloving husband. Sadly, six sons and one daughter later, we all know the outcome of Leah's failed efforts.

But now that attachment would be a deep spiritual connection that would link the Levites to God. The Levites were the only tribe who had not taken part in the mayhem that invaded the Sinai camp. Subsequently, they would be the only tribe to join Aaron and his sons in the priesthood (Num. 1:50). Perhaps as Aaron and his sons were being trained in the wilderness seminary to become priests, the lessons they learned were passed down to their brothers at home. It is conceivable that while Aaron and his sons prepared for daily worship, the remaining Levites in the community were exposed to the practice of following God's worship commands. I can imagine the Levites singing praise and worshiping in their homes, while they were preparing to offer the daily morning and evening sacrifice. Maybe their sincere worship practice spread throughout the entire house. Everyone would be excited when it was time for their family priest to prepare his heart and mind to offer the daily sacrifice. Your worship to God should always begin at home. The first conversions for every Levite should take place first in his own heart and then in his own home.

So I imagine other Levites may have been influenced by the spiritual leadership that surrounded their families. I think it is fair to conclude that as the Aaronic priests served God, their leadership influence flowed beyond the bounds of their immediate families to the entire Levite tribe. This process of spiritual influence made the Levites leaders. Ken Blanchard, author of the *One Minute Manager,* states this concept simply: "What is leadership? It's an influence process."[4]

What type of leaders were the Levites? God called the Levites to serve Aaron and the congregation (Num. 3:6–7). When your leadership is based on your commitment to serve others, this makes you a servant leader. Robert Greenleaf, an early contributor to the discussion of servant leadership, explains, "A servant leader must attend to the needs of followers and help them become healthier, wiser, and more willing to accept their responsibilities. The servant leader must stand for what is good and right.... Social injustice and inequality should be opposed whenever possible."[5]

The Levites were called to serve God that day by correcting the spiritual injustice that had infected the tribes. Therefore a battle would be fought among brothers. At God's command, Moses told the Levites to go throughout the camp and kill their brothers (Exod. 32:27). The Levites chose to serve God no matter what the cost. Through Moses, God commanded the Levites to separate themselves and kill all the guilty offenders. Now God Himself would divide the Israelites by separating the faithful from the faithless, the repentant from the rebellious, and the saint from the sinner. God consecrated and blessed the Levites due to their obedience (Exod. 32:29). Afterward, the Levites became the servants to the priests and spiritual worship leaders for Israel (Num. 3:12–13). God's protection and priesthood for the Levites became an everlasting covenant (Deut. 12:19; 1 Chron. 15:2).

Like the Levites, it is the time for you to make your choice. As a worshiper, you have heard the music playing from both sides of divergent cultural camps as you stand in the valley of spiritual decision. So like Moses, I am making a clarion call to you today.

I am calling you and all true worshipers like you from around the world. Tell me, who is on the Lord's side? Will *you* take *your* stand and pledge to become a spiritual Levite today? Will you pledge to remain in close communion with God so that you know the sound of true musical praise? Will you choose to be on God's side and live by His biblical standards, or will you in ignorance play music on Satan's side and be lured by his seductions? Will you remain in the valley and continue to offer your worship to the idol of praise music? Or will you stand strong on the mountaintop with God and refuse to be held captive by the sweeping sands of spiritual drift found in today's Christian music culture? I challenge you choose today whom you will serve! Choose the path of biblical praise; choose God's side!

One thing I know for certain: if you choose the Lord's side, it will be a difficult and dangerous journey. Choosing God's side in praise is never popular or easy. Like the ancient Levites, you will be in the minority. You may have to separate yourself from some of your brothers and sisters to continue to live a holy life and listen to what is right. Your words of truth may seem to cut and kill their carefree spirits. Although the divine division will be difficult, the rewards for being on God's side are bountiful and eternal. I can assure you that your life of true worship in Jesus Christ will transform you. You will never be the same! So I invite you to join me on this deeper praise journey to explore the biblical foundations and methods for offering true praise.

LEVITE LESSONS

1. Develop a relationship with God that results in deep
   spiritual maturity. Then you will be able to discern
   the one and only side in the worship wars–God's side.

2. In true praise, we united our sacred songs of praise to worship the one true God, our Lord and Savior Jesus Christ.

3. Without Scripture to guide and formulate our opinions, we worship in vain.

4. Do not be a praise *worrier* who lives to fight others. Be a praise *warrior* who fights for the cause of Christ yet lives surrendered to God.

5. Our worship should begin at home. The first conversions for every Levite should take place in our own heart and then in our own home.

6. Levites are servant leaders who choose to worship God no matter what the cost.

PRACTICAL PRAISE QUESTION

How can I begin to apply these lessons to my own praise life today?

(Read and sign Levite Pledge in Appendix I.)

(For more information on the Levites refer to my first book, *Levite Praise: God's Biblical Design for Praise and Worship.*)

ENDNOTES

1. *Blue Letter Bible,* s.v. "qowl," https://www.blueletterbible.org/lang/lexicon/lexicon.cfm?Strongs=H6963&t=kjv, accessed September 6, 2012.

2. *Blue Letter Bible,* s.v., "`anah," https://www.blueletterbible.org/lang/lexicon/lexicon.cfm?Strongs=H6031, accessed September 6, 2012.

3. *Blue Letter Bible,* s.v., "shachath," https://www.blueletterbible.org/lang/lexicon/lexicon.cfm?strongs=H7843, accessed September 27, 2012.

4. Ken Blanchard, quoted in James C. Hunter, *The World's Most Powerful Leadership Principle: How to Become a Servant Leader* (New York: Crown Business, 2004), 47.

5. Robert K. Greenleaf, *The Servant-Leader Within: A Transformative Path* (New York: Paulist Press, 2003).

Chapter 2

TOTAL PRAISE

All the earth shall worship You and sing praises to You;
they shall sing praises to Your name. Selah.

—Psalm 66:4

Pure Praise

*I*N THE COOL morning breeze, the birds sang sweet melodies of praise to their Creator. The rising sunlight warmed the awakening earth, while the low hum of the insects and the movement of the cattle blended in a rhythmic symphony that gently aroused David. Each morning, David inhaled the delightful aroma of the figs, olives, and grapes that would grow near the cornfields in the verdant valley of his hometown Bethlehem. At daybreak, David would begin happily tending to his father's flocks. He loved the solitude of Bethlehem's rolling hills and grassy plains. Every day, God enveloped David in the luminous light of His love through the picturesque landscape of nature. David felt the constancy of God's love through nature's tender kiss. It was in the fields, this place of fellowship with God, that his heart sang. David was a devout and diligent worshiper. He began each new day in sacred conversation and intimate communion with God as he conducted his humble yet noble work as a shepherd. Pure praise emerges from a personal relationship with God that depends upon and deepens in daily solitude and meditation (Ps. 36:9; 92:5).

The Prophet Samuel began his day as usual, at the Lord's command. God told Samuel, "Fill your horn with oil and be on your way; I am sending you to Jesse of Bethlehem. I have chosen one of his sons to be king" (1 Sam. 16:1, NIV). Today, Samuel was to anoint a new king. God had commanded that he take a heifer to Bethlehem for a sacrifice and wait for His approval on the man that would replace King Saul. As Samuel entered the city, he invited the elders of the town, along with David's father Jesse and his seven sons, to the sacrifice. But first they all had to be sanctified and consecrated (1 Sam. 16:5). In order to do God's work, we must become sanctified, set apart, and holy in our hearts and minds.

As Samuel saw Jesse's first son Eliab, he was impressed by his stature and handsome appearance. He believed that surely Eliab was the Lord's choice for king. But the Lord said to Samuel, "Do not look at his appearance or at his physical stature, because I have refused him. *For the LORD does not see as man sees;* for man looks at the outward appearance, but the LORD looks at the heart" (1 Sam. 16:7). Six sons later, God still had not chosen a king. Samuel was surprised but knew God's command. He could not finish his work until the new king was anointed. Samuel asked Jesse if he had any more sons. Then Jesse mentioned that his youngest son David was in the pasture with the sheep.

How often do we select artists as worship leaders based on the outward appearance of their musical talents or popularity? It is essential to follow God's model when you choose someone as worship pastor, minister of music, music director, worship leader, choir director, band leader, pianist, or any leadership role within the music department. Do not choose a person solely based on their musical talent or acclaim. Believe me, this course that has become so common in our churches is a recipe for spiritual disaster. Mere musical talent is never enough! God's selection of a praise leader is not determined by how well a person can sing or play an instrument—or how charismatic they are. Giftedness is the last attribute on God's soul-searching artist list.

Where is the model or list found for God's artist selection? I thought you would never ask! It is found in the Book of Exodus. When God selected an artist to build and design the wilderness tabernacle, He made a list of seven spiritual characteristics. Exodus 31:2–3, 6 reads,

> See, I have *called* by name Bezalel the son of Uri, the son of Hur, of the tribe of Judah. And I have *filled him with the Spirit* of God, in *wisdom*, in *understanding*, in *knowledge*, and in all manner of workmanship.... And I, indeed I, have *appointed* with him Aholiab the son of Ahisamach, of the tribe of Dan; and I have put wisdom in the hearts of all the *gifted* artisans, that they may make all that I have commanded you.

In these texts, God declares that Bezalel and Aholiab had seven spiritual characteristics.

The Lord's artists Bezalel and Aholiab were:

1. Called by God
2. Filled with the Spirit
3. Possessing wisdom
4. Possessing understanding
5. Possessing knowledge
6. Appointed
7. Gifted

On God's artist list, giftedness is last, yes, even least! Yet on our artist lists, giftedness is the *only* attribute we seem to measure. Do you use God's standards to select a musical leader? Are the people that you select to sing songs of praise first *called* by God and then *filled* with His Holy Spirit? Do they possess *wisdom, understanding,* and *knowledge* about offering God pure praise? Have they been *appointed* by God and other spiritual leaders who affirm their ability to lead people to Jesus Christ through music? God looks into the heart of every person that He calls to see if they are His devoted followers. God examines whether or not they have a knowledge of His Holy Word. He searches the heart to see if he or she is set on living a life in total love, obedience, and commitment to Him.

As simple as it may seem to understand God's standards, there is more than what is apparent to us on the surface. To fully comprehend God's guidelines, we must delve deeper. We must be clear on God's definition of wisdom, understanding, and knowledge. The Hebrew word used for wisdom (*chokmah*) means "skill (in war), wisdom (in administration), shrewdness, prudence (in religious affairs), wisdom (ethical and religious).[1] The Hebrew word used for understanding (*tabuwn*) describes understanding as a skill, but then adds intelligence, insight, and teacher to complete the definition.[2] Finally, the Hebrew word used for knowledge (*da'ath*) continues to build on skill, understanding, and wisdom, and then includes perception and discernment to the list.[3] Wow, now we see clearly what God requires for artistry that is ministry! God's artists are much more than merely talented and gifted!

As church musicians, we must possess wisdom, knowledge, and understanding. These attributes produce musical skill which will enable us to do spiritual warfare, provide leadership through a vision which embraces biblical truth, execute music management, be sharp in practical matters, offer ethical judgment, and teach through the intuition of the Holy Spirit. Seven is the number in the Bible that is symbolic of completion and perfection (Gen. 2:1–3). These seven spiritual characteristics are required of the person who God appoints and gifts with creative talents. This is how we can completely use our artistry in God's perfect will for ministry.

Once you have met God's characteristic criteria, then you are qualified to be a spiritual music leader. God's selected spiritual music leaders are those who have first surrendered their souls, and then use their giftedness in song to lead His people. In all fairness, I hear you asking yourself, "How can I be held accountable for something I did not know?" Well, that is a good question. God is just, wonderful, and gracious to us all. He winks at our ignorance (Acts 17:30, KJV). He does not hold us accountable for what we do not know. But since you have read this chapter, you are no longer ignorant. Now you know God's model! Therefore you can begin to *prayerfully* and *carefully* apply this principle *first to yourself* and then to others.

Practical Praise

As David sat quietly, pondering God's goodness and caring for his sheep, he noticed two figures in the distance. One was familiar. It was his father Jesse. But the other stately figure seemed to walk with a singular purpose. David quickly recognized it was the Prophet Samuel who had joined his father. Thinking that they may have come to select a lamb for the sacrifice, David pulled the herd's finest firstborn male lamb closer to his side. He had cared for the sheep so tenderly that he was confident there was an unblemished lamb for the Prophet Samuel to add to the heifer for his sacrifice.

Jesse beckoned David, and he came quickly. As the youngest of Jesse's eight sons, David was not yet the most handsome of his brothers. Nor was he considered old enough to be a valorous man of war. However, David was a young man of duty and responsibility. It was his service to care for his father's sheep. David took this work very seriously. He would even lay down his life to protect any one of his beloved sheep. He had proven his might more than once as he bravely fought off both the lion and the bear to protect his flock. In the pastures, David had become a young man of principle, valor, and great integrity.

As Samuel sat with Jesse awaiting David's arrival, he saw God's favor beaming from David's face as he came closer. David was ruddy, bright eyed, and handsome. God said to Samuel, "Up on your feet! Anoint him! This is the one!" (1 Sam. 16:12, THE MESSAGE). Oh, if only people could see God's favor on our faces and in our lives. If only we would allow God's holiness to shine in and through us. Instead we are most comfortable determining the power of praise by the music that we hear and feel not by our lives of holiness and faith.

David was a lowly shepherd of his father's flock. Now, because of his relationship of pure praise to God, he was called to lead. David would shepherd his heavenly Father's flock and become king of His beloved nation of Israel. "Then Samuel took the horn of oil and anointed him in the midst of his brothers; and the Spirit of the LORD came upon David from that day forward" (1 Sam 16:13). So let's check off the first two items on God's artist list. David was *called* by God and *filled with the Holy Spirit*. From the pasture, this young, lowly shepherd was called to be a spiritual leader who would pastor the Lord's flock (Ps. 78:70–72).

You know, I have noticed that there is something unique about shepherding that draws one into a closer personal relationship with God. The patriarchs, Abraham, Isaac, and Jacob, were shepherds. Moses became a shepherd in preparation to deliver the Israelites. As a boy, David was a shepherd. Then finally, our Lord and Savior Jesus Christ humbled Himself to be born in a manger among the sheep; He is our Shepherd (Ps. 23:1). For the worship leader, there are significant, practical lessons to be learned from the role of a shepherd.

The shepherd's role required ruling over and guiding the sheep under his care. The shepherd was to feed, nourish, and provide ample amounts of water for the sheep to thrive. For the sheep to live, he had to find good pasture. The shepherd was to guard his sheep from predators and spend enough time with them to be sensitive to their daily needs. His or her job was to provide care and promote healing if perchance one of his sheep was attacked by a wild animal (Gen. 29:9). He would use oil to cover the sheep's wounds, and then he would nurse it back to good health. Also the shepherd was to be a warrior who would risk his own life to protect his sheep from any wild beast that may threaten the flock. It is no coincidence that the Greek word for *pastor, poimēn* (4166), is defined as "a shepherd, one who tends herds or flocks (not merely one who feeds them). 'Pastors' guide as well as feed flocks (Acts 20:28). This involves tender care and vigilant superintendence (1 Pet. 5: 1–2)."[4] Good shepherds pastor their flock!

God is looking for the good shepherds among us who will pastor His flocks with musical praise. As God's worship leader, you must be *pastoral* with the ministration of your musical gifts and the talents and giftings of the people God has called you to lead. Does this mean that you must immediately quit your job, enroll in the nearest seminary, and become a full-time pastor? Well, I say yes, only if you feel that is God's specific call on your life. However, being *pastoral* with your musical talents means more than a seminary degree. It means that you are leading and guiding people toward the gospel of Jesus Christ while guarding and protecting them from the wiles of the devil through the ministry of music. Jesus Christ is the good shepherd who will empower us to do the formidable work that allows us to lead, guide, and protect His sheep (John 10:11).

How can you accomplish all this with mere music? Well, music that is filled with pure praise is saturated by the anointing oil of Holy Spirit power! To unleash this power, you must be capable of expressing God's mission and vision through music. This type of music will offer a biblical and spiritual message to undergird every aspect and segment of the worship service. Just as a pastor selects his sermons, your songs of praise should be chosen to feed the spiritual needs of your church members. Your songs should reach the hearts and minds of the people you serve with the gospel message and not be shallowly based on personal preference or the popular worship hits of the day. In *Music and Ministry: A Biblical Counterpoint,* Calvin Johansson writes, "The church needs musicians who know what church music should express and who also understand the musical methodology for expressing it."[5] This means that for us to use music with pastoral power, the theology (words) and the melody (music) must match to enable the infilling of the Holy Spirit. Therefore, praise is a unique art form that requires spiritual knowledge, wisdom, and understanding.

Also, like a shepherd, you must make it your duty to know the spiritual and emotional needs of your sheep in order to engage them with God through musical praise. In his book *The Most Powerful*

Leadership Principle, James Hunter tells us that "legitimate leadership influence is built upon serving, sacrificing, and seeking the greatest good of those being led."[6] As you lead, your relationship with God will now extend to the members you are called to serve. It is your responsibility to get to know your church's spiritual condition. You can do this in a number of ways. You can schedule regular meetings with your pastor and the church elders—or develop your own personal relationship with various ministry leaders and members. As a pastoral worship leader, you will forge a relationship with God and man—not man and music. Music is the method we use to lead people to Christ. Your Christ-focused connection to convert souls and minister to hearts will enable you to feed your members as a Spirit-filled worship leader.

Finally, shepherding the flock with praise requires a warrior mentality. We are in spiritual warfare against wicked satanic forces (Eph. 6:12). Like a great warrior, you must be selective and protective with your music so that you can guard your flock from the negative influences that may ultimately lead them astray. If some negative influences seep in, then you must know how to apply the healing balm of the Bible to cure all spiritual ills. This is how your praise music will wage war against the devil. When your music is watered with the Word of God and permeated by Holy Spirit power, demons have to flee (1 Sam. 16:23)! No weapon formed against you shall prosper (Isa. 54:17).

When you follow this model, each song that you select for the church service will be a power-packed musical sermon. The songs that are chosen throughout the entire worship service will contain a music ministry message that is overflowing with Holy Spirit power. Our praise and worship sets, response songs, special music selections, altar calls, and congregational hymns will all be rooted and grounded in the good pasture of God's Holy Word. Then our songs will specifically cater to the spiritual needs of the congregations we serve. If we follow these biblical principles, we will gain and maintain the spiritual maturity needed to guard our hearts and minds while we lead others towards Jesus Christ and away from the devil's deceptions. By utilizing God's guidelines, we will develop a deep spiritual conviction that will enable us to fight and win the raging wars that have seeped into our worship.

DEFINITION OF PRAISE

Although David was called as a leader, he was also a master musician. He met God's seventh spiritual characteristic because he was *gifted*. David's musical talents and exceptional skill for singing, songwriting, and playing the harp were renowned throughout all Israel—so much so that when King Saul was plagued with a distressing spirit from the Lord, David was appointed to serve Saul because of his musical talent. He was lauded for his other keen spiritual attributes however (1 Sam.16:18). In the fields and throughout his life, David would sing and pen songs that reflected his personal experiences. David extolled the majesty of God, the beauty of nature, the history of Israel, and his vast triumphant and tragic life experiences. Praise to God was his purpose for being.

So I cannot write a book about praise and neglect to define the word *praise* from a biblical perspective. The most frequently used Hebrew word for praise, *hālal,* means the following:

> ...to praise, celebrate, glory, sing (praise), boast. The meaning "to praise" is actually the meaning of the intensive form of the Hebrew verb *hālal,* which in its simple active form means "to boast." The word is found in the Ugaritic in the sense of "shouting," and perhaps "jubilation." The word *hālal* is found more than 160 times in the Old Testament. The Hebrew name for the book of Psalms is simply the equivalent of the word "praises." Psalms 113–118 are traditionally referred to as the Hallel Psalms. Scholars agree this was the hymn sung by Jesus when he instituted the Last Supper (Matt. 26:30). The word *hālal* is the source of "Hallelujah," a Hebrew expression of

"praise" to God which has been taken over into virtually every language of mankind.[7]

Many times we hear the refrain, "Hallelujah is the highest praise." Well, it is! This phrase of praise maintains its unique stature among praise words because it contains the glorious name of God. The term *Hallelujah* literally means "Let us praise Yah." The word *Yah* is the shortened form of Yahweh, the hallowed Israelite name for God (Isa. 26:4). Therefore, when we shout "hallelu-jah," we literally cry out in a universal, earthly, and heavenly language: "Let us praise God" (Rev. 19:1–4). As we exclaim *hallelujah*, we give praise to Jehovah God the Highest.

There are eighteen words translated for praise in the Bible (eleven are in Hebrew and seven in Greek). Our acts of praise differ from our worship offering. As you can imagine with so many words, *praise* has many definitions. Bob Sorge's book *Exploring Worship* provides this practical definition:

> Praise is preoccupied with who God is and what he has done. It focuses on both his incomparable character and his wondrous acts on behalf of his children. When God does something glorious for us, we love to lift high his praises. And yet praise is not simply our thankful response to his provision; praise is also very fitting even when we have no specific gift of God in mind. He is worthy to be praised solely for who he is.[8]

The Holman Bible Dictionary defines praise as "one of humanity's many responses to God's revelation of Himself."[9] Therefore, if praise is how we respond to seeing God, then we must assume when we see Him, we are in His holy presence. So our praise must have a specific approach. Think of it this way. As a tourist, if you want to visit the president of the United States, you could go to Washington, DC, and see the White House on an impromptu visit. You could walk up to 1600 Pennsylvania Avenue, stand on the street corner, and see the White House without any mandatory preparation or viewing restrictions. But if you want to make a personal visit to meet the president or tour the inside of the White House, that is a very different story. Before you can meet the president, there are requirements that must be followed. This includes writing a letter to your member of Congress at the U.S. Capitol to make a formal written request up to six months or no less than twenty-one days in advance. But once you have met the requirements, the White House tour is free of charge. You can meet the President and First Lady, shake their hands, show your admiration, and personally thank them for all they have done for you as a citizen of this country.

Praise to God is very similar. As a new believer, coming to God the Father is simple and requires only the desire to see Him and be in His presence. But first, we must have an encounter with Jesus Christ because we cannot see God unless we go through Jesus (John 14:6). But when we accept Jesus Christ, then we can enter into God's presence. Once we are in God's presence, then there are certain ways that we should respond to please Him and proclaim His goodness in our lives. Since only God is our Creator, Redeemer, Sustainer and Deliver, our response of praise is how we thank Him for His goodness toward us. Because of His grace, we have become heirs to the throne. Jesus paid it all. He paid the price for us on the cross at Calvary. So now heaven is free of charge! We can enter boldly to the throne (Heb. 4:16). Every one of us who engage in genuine praise will one day become citizens of heaven (Phil. 3:20). But to enjoy these privileges, we must enter into God's presence in the way that He prescribes. Only then He will accept our deepest gratitude, love, and reverence. Since God inhabits our praise (Ps. 22:3), then praise enables us to experience an intimate face-to-face relationship with God (Ps. 27:8).

Praise is beautiful, and God our divine Creator loves variety (Ps. 147:1). God's love for variety can be seen throughout the beauty of nature in all of creation. God's passion for variety extends to worship too. God infuses His sovereign character and affection for variety into the way He desires us to praise Him. David understood these praise principles thoroughly and applied this faithful formula to his musicianship, leadership, and life. Because of his profound ability to give God glory through a life devoted to praise, David earned the respected title "man after God's own heart" (1 Sam. 13:14). He also showed that he had godly *wisdom* even in adversity (1 Sam. 18:14), another one of God's seven spiritual characteristics. The *Holman Bible Dictionary* states that the modes of praise are many. However, it includes seven modes of praise to God.

SEVEN MODES OF PRAISE

1. *Offering a Sacrifice:* In ancient worship, the priests would sacrifice a lamb as the daily offering (Exod. 29:38). Today, we no longer need a lamb to slaughter for our sins, since Jesus Christ became the Lamb of God who takes away the world's sins (John 1:29). So in our deepest praise, we offer ourselves, our lives to God. David understood this principle and noted in Ps. 40:6, 8–9 that his sacrifice of praise was not burnt or sin offerings but the law within his heart that he expressed with his lips. We must offer ourselves as living sacrifices, holy and pleasing to God—which is our spiritual worship (Rom. 12:1, NIV).

2. *Physical Movement:* Bible history confirms that the Israelites were expressive in their praise to God. In Israelite worship, the Israelites would engage in various movements. They would stand, bow, prostrate themselves, dance, clap, kneel, and lift their hands. In Nehemiah 8:5–6 we see some examples of these praise movements (standing, bowing, prostration, lifting hands). In Psalm 134:2; 141:2, David instructs us to lift our hands in the sanctuary and bless the Lord as the evening sacrifice. David

danced before the Lord (2 Sam. 6:14) as an offering
of praise. The psalm writer instructs us to clap our
hands in praise (Ps. 47:1). Even though this praise
act is mentioned in the Bible, some theologians
view clapping as eschatological—only acceptable for
King Jesus' Second Coming—and not church worship. I assert there is a present-day praise application because in each praise and worship experience
we make Jesus king over our lives and ask Him to
come into our hearts.

Nevertheless, the application of these praise movements is dependent on the congregation that you
serve. Whether you use one or all of these movements in worship, it is your act of praise that pleases
God. Not everyone has to respond in the same exact
way for our praise movements to be acceptable.
Remember, we must be wise and understanding with
our praise. God loves variety. Therefore, the movements that elicit praise for your congregation may
differ from movements that elicit praise for mine. The
movements that evoke praise for me may differ from
the ones that evoke praise for you! That does not
make my praise movements wrong and yours right or
vice versa. This just underscores the variety ingrained
in God's kingdom. Any physical movement within
these prescribed parameters is all God requires from
us for proper praise. Hallelujah!

3. *Silence and Meditation:* We live in a world filled
   with the hustle and bustle of activity. As Christians
   we should learn to cherish and create meditative moments of silence. We must build in times of
   silence into our lives and worship services. The word
   Selah is most frequently used in the Book of Psalms,

and three times in the Book of Habakkuk. *Selah* is a musical notation that means "to pause and think calmly on what has just been expressed."[10] Silence and meditation are an essential part of praise (Ps. 77:12). It is in the quiet times that we can hear the still, small voice of God (1 Kings 19:11–12).

4. *Testimony:* How can others know how wondrous God has been in our lives if we neglect to share our life experiences through stories? Testimonies about God's goodness are tools we can used to strengthen our faith and encourage others to trust and praise God no matter how difficult the situation (Ps. 105:1–2). Testimonies should be used in the church as a means to extol God's goodness, express our faith, build community, and promote compassion for others.

5. *Prayer:* Prayer provides us with constant communication with God. We can pray anytime and anywhere. Prayer is a conduit to the halls of heaven and a pathway into God's presence. David knew that in God's presence there is life, pleasure, and fullness of joy (Ps. 16:11). Isaiah 56:7 reads, "For My house shall be called a house of prayer for all nations." David assures us that our prayers of praise are a sacrifice that ascend to God Himself, saying, "Let my prayer be set before You as incense" (Ps. 141: 2; Rev. 5:8).

6. *A Holy Life:* God continues to admonish us to be holy. Why? Because He is holy (Lev. 19:2; Ps. 86:2; 1 Thess. 4:7). Praise allows us to reflect the character of our Creator. Through constant praise, we become transformed. We cannot encounter God and remain the same. "But you are a chosen generation, a royal priesthood, a holy nation, His own special people,

that you may proclaim the praises of Him who called
you out of darkness into His marvelous light" (1 Pet.
2:9). When we bless God in praise, we are bathed in
the light of God's presence (Ps. 104:1–2).

7. *Music:* Music, both vocal and instrumental,
pleases God.

> Music is audible, melodious adoration that God created for His perpetual praise (Rev. 5:8–9).

God instructs His people
to sing and rejoice around
Him (Zech. 2:10). It is widely
recognized that most praise
words can be linked with
vocal and / or instrumental music. Music has God-
ordained prophetic power. David made instruments
for giving praise (1 Chron. 23:5). First Chronicles
25:1 reads, "David also separated for the service
some of the sons of Asaph and Jeduthun who should
prophesy with harps, stringed instruments and cymbals." The Lord Himself chooses to show His delight
in us through music and will rejoice over us with
singing (Zeph. 3:17). In heaven, the redeemed will
sing with the harps of God (Rev. 15:3). Praise music
transforms behavior. In *Ancient Psalms and Modern
Worship,* Edward M. Curtis cites Ronald Allen and
Dr. Gordon Borror, who coauthored *Worship: Redis-
covering the Missing Jewel:* "An idea (either good or
bad) set to a good melody, given rhythmic inten-
sity and harmonic consistency, can really work its
way into our minds…music is a powerful way to
get…ideas implanted and affect the behavior of mankind.…What we sing we remember, because we have
combined the power of intellect with emotion."[11]

It doesn't matter how beautiful your melodies or wonderful your music. It makes no difference how talented you are or how much popularity you may have. It does not matter if *you* think your praise is genuine. Your music and worship could be of the highest and holiest genre (according to you). But believe me, if it is focused on fame and personal satisfaction, it is worthless. Your praise is pure mayhem. Instead of the tender touch of a love relationship with God, your praise becomes harsh and hollow like sounding brass and tinkling cymbals. Your praise and worship is just chaos and displeasing *noise* to God if it is not covered by the blood of Jesus Christ!

When we bicker, fight, and complain about the music, our offerings of praise are not covered by the blood of Jesus Christ; instead, they may be soiled by the sin of our self-serving pride. There is a way to give God glorious praise. No matter what we offer God, it is sinful because we are all sinners (Rom. 3:23). But if we give Jesus Christ our hearts, then He will cover our praise with His righteousness. Our praise becomes a sweet melody to God because it is saturated by the blood of Jesus Christ and His Holy Word (John 1:1). We must shift our praise paradigm, return to God's Holy Word, and be revived by the revelation of His truth. Calvin Johansson agrees. He writes, "If theology is to be the foundation of our value system, then clearly the musician's regard for musical art cannot be allowed to become idolatrous. By the same token, methods will not be worshiped; rather, they will be determined by theological presuppositions. Music directors will not bow at the shrine of success. There will be no conflict between artistry, spirituality, and methodology."[12]

Deuteronomy 29:29 reads, "The secret things belong to the LORD our God, but those things which are revealed belong to us and to our children forever, that we may do all the words of this law." I pray that these truths that have been revealed to you today will become a path to your promise to give God total praise.

LEVITE LESSONS

1. Pure praise emerges from a personal relationship with God that depends upon and deepens in daily solitude and meditation (Ps. 36:9; Ps. 92:5).

2. In order to do God's work, we must become sanctified, set apart, and holy in our hearts and minds.

3. Giftedness is the last attribute on God's soul searching artist list (Exod. 31:2–3, 6).

4. As God's worship leader you must be *pastoral* with the ministration of your musical gifts and the talents and gifting of the people God has called you to lead.

5. Praise is a unique art form that requires spiritual knowledge, wisdom, and understanding.

6. God infuses His sovereign character and affection for variety into the way He desires us to praise Him.

7. We must shift our praise paradigm, return to God's Holy Word, and be revived by the revelation of His truth (Deut. 29:29).

PRACTICAL PRAISE QUESTION

What steps can you take today to apply these lessons to your church's music ministry department or worship service?

ENDNOTES

1. *Blue Letter Bible,* s.v. "chokmah," https://www.blueletterbible.org/lang/lexicon/lexicon.cfm?Strongs=H2451&t=KJV, accessed October 4, 2015.

2. *Blue Letter Bible,* s.v. "tabuwn," https://www.blueletterbible.org/lang/lexicon/lexicon.cfm?Strongs=H8394&t=KJV, accessed on October 4, 2015.

3. *Blue Letter Bible,* s.v. "da'ath" https://www.blueletterbible.org/lang/lexicon/lexicon.cfm?Strongs=H1847&t=KJV, accessed on October 4, 2015.

4. W.E. Vine, Merrill F. Unger, and William White Jr., *Vines's Complete Expository Dictionary of Old and New Testament Words* (Nashville, TN: Thomas Nelson, 1996), 462.

5. Calvin M. Johansson, *Music & Ministry: A Biblical Counterpoint,* 2nd ed. (Peabody, MA: Hendrickson Publishers, Inc., 1998), 56.

6. James C. Hunter, *The Most Powerful Leadership Principle: How to Become a Servant Leader* (New York: Crown Business, 2004), 73.

7. Vine, Unger, and White, 184–185.

8. Bob Sorge, *Exploring Worship: A Practical Guide to Praise and Worship* (Lee's Summit, MO: Oasis House, 2001), 2.

9. Chad Brand, Charles Draper, Archie England, eds., *Holman Illustrated Bible Dictionary* (Nashville, TN: Holman Bible Publishers, 2001), 1319.

10. *Blue Letter Bible,* s.v., "celah," https://www.blueletterbible.org/lang/lexicon/lexicon.cfm?strongs=H5542, accessed October 24, 2012.

11. Quoted in Edward M. Curtis, *Ancient Psalms and Modern Worship* (Evangelical Theological Society Papers, 1992), 285–96.

12. Johansson, 7.

Chapter 3

ORDINARY PEOPLE

For God is the King of all the earth;
sing praises with understanding.
—PSALM 47:7

UNDERSTANDING PRAISE

*A*LTHOUGH DAVID'S LIFE was a towering tale of magnificent triumphs and multiple tragedies, he remained faithful to God and a humble servant to men. Even after his prestigious *appointment* to King Saul's royal court as his private musician and personal armor bearer, David was able to balance his prominent positions with his ordinary life. David stayed faithful to his father Jesse and still traveled home on occasions to feed his sheep (1 Sam. 17:15). One day while at home, Jesse asked David to take lunch to his brothers at their camp where the Israelite army was fighting the Philistines. David obeyed. But when he arrived and heard the brazen taunts of the Philistine's champion warrior, the giant Goliath, he was outraged.

He questioned his older brother Eliab, "Who is this uncircumcised Philistine, that he should defy the armies of the living God?" (1 Sam. 17:26). After listening to another series of Goliath's blasphemous speeches, David became furious! He did not care that Goliath stood 9 feet 9 inches tall. It did not matter to him that Goliath had frightened all the bravest men in the Israelite army by railing threats against them. It made no difference that he was not a soldier and just a youth. David's fastened his mind on the power of the living God and became indignant at anyone who dared to defy Him!

David's faith in God and feats of valor in the field with his father's sheep had filled him with spiritual courage. This enabled David to wield his slingshot and single-handedly throw one stone that hit Goliath square in the forehead and killed him (1 Sam. 17:49). Then David cut off Goliath's head with one swift strike of the giant's own sword. David's reliance on God's power and righteous indignation freed the nation of Israel. Since David behaved *wisely* and courageously he received a tremendous reward. He became a national military hero, supervised the royal army, and was admired by the servants in King Saul's court. He never returned home to his father's house again (1 Sam.18:2, 5).

How many of us can be called wise and courageous because we know how to balance our Christian faith with worldly fame? It seems like in today's music industry whirlwind, being a popular worship leader has become the sure path to success and superstardom. Sadly, some of us crave the spotlight and are starved for fame. Many times, we receive accolades as singers and musicians that are tremendous. We may even attain local, national, or worldwide recording acclaim. But do we as godly artists have the restraint to resist feeding our egos with a gluttonous appetite for worldly fame and fortune? Do we have the wisdom and courage to constantly live in Christ and proclaim our faith? Or do we fall prey to Satan's subtle suggestion that my songs, not my lifestyle represent my deep spiritual beliefs and devotion to God? Do we immerse ourselves in Scripture before our worship sets, or are we more worried about our image and wardrobe? Are we soldiers of the Cross or sellouts to the crowds?

We need godly wisdom and spiritual understanding to navigate this culture's constant lust for worldly fame. Our worship will venture deep into the hearts of men when it is overflowing with the Word of God. Then we can stand in the flood of man's praise and see only God as the source of our pride (Ps. 35:18). In the spotlight of fame, we will not become greedy for personal glory. Even the accolades of men will become another form of praise to God and not a personal praise party. Although God uses ordinary people, being an artist for God is no ordinary task! We must keep our worship focused on the kingdom of God and not the pleasures of this world. Spiritual artistry requires a strict diet of righteousness, love, peace, and joy in the Holy Spirit that is acceptable to God and approved by men (Rom. 14:17–18).

God uses ordinary people because
God desires extraordinary praise.

Although the angels and heavenly host serenade God eternally (Rev. 5:8–10), He still longs to accept our love songs of praise. He yearns to hear the song of praise that only we who are redeemed can sing (Rev. 14:3). Therefore, God is not interested in your songs if they are just offered with surface sincerity. God is not impressed by your real or perceived superstar status. He does not wish for you to travel your region or even the world to be the most sought-after worship leader with the highest record sales on the Christian music charts. God longs for our hearts of love in genuine praise to Him. God desires to dwell in our midst as we rejoice and sing His praise (Zech. 2:10). He longs to spend eternity with us and give us a crown of life. He desires that our praise songs reflect His character so they will penetrate deep into the hearts of our listeners. God wants our worship to feed the soul and quench the sinner's spiritual thirst.

David *understood* his purpose in life. He knew it was not to be famous. He was not a vain glory seeker who was strung out on his national fame as a singer and songwriter. David's purpose was to live a life of love and obedience in devoted praise to God. He did this in every area in which he served. David was a committed God-seeker. He completely understood that his blessings did not come from his ability to praise, but from seeking the God who is our praise (Deut. 10:21). Do we have the same understanding today? Are we focused on praise music to build our faith, or is praise music the ticket to establish our fame? God will give you the desires of your heart if you *first seek* Him and His kingdom (Matt. 6:33). Without a laser focus on the righteousness of Jesus Christ and bearing fruit through faith, all praise will become dry, self-centered, and spiritually unproductive. Without a focus on faith in God instead of worldly fame, your praise will lack the flow of the Holy Spirit that is like a fountain of water springing up into everlasting life (John 4:14).

Like most good things that end, David's time of fame and fortune was fleeting. It was not long before the evil spirit that plagued King Saul again reared its ugly head. It infected his love and admiration for David, turning it into fear, resentment, and jealousy. As the Israelite army returned home victorious from defeating the Philistines, the women of the cities came out to greet King Saul with joy. They were singing, dancing, and playing tambourines and musical instruments. They sang a song as they danced and said, "Saul has slain his thousands, and David his ten thousands" (1 Sam. 18:6–7). Then Saul heard their praise and became jealous. I can imagine he thought to himself—*the nerve of my subjects! They only credit me with a thousand and David with ten thousands! "Now, what more can he have but the kingdom?"* (1 Sam. 18:8). So Saul became angry and envious of David because the Lord was with him and the people loved him.

The next day Saul tried to kill David by throwing a spear at him during his routine serenade. David escaped twice from Saul's murderous schemes. So Saul removed David from his presence by making him captain over a thousand field soldiers. Despite it all, David remained wise. While he served in the field, all Israel and Judah came to love him (1 Sam. 18:14, 16). Soon afterward, Saul tried to murder David again while he was serenading him (1 Sam. 19:10). But this time David escaped and fled from the palace at night. He went to his home where his wife Michal hid him. But Saul sent messengers to his home so David had to flee. This situation was the beginning of more than a decade of David being persecuted and relentlessly hunted by Saul. In a day, David went from national hero to public enemy No. 1 (1 Sam. 20:1). It is ironic that it was a song that improved David's life and brought him favor and a position in Saul's palace. Yet it was also a song that ruined David's life and made him flee from Saul's presence. But this is not uncommon. Songs can have either positive or negative effects on any ordinary person. Would you agree? A song can change your life!

In history, we can trace the wide range of life-changing effects songs have had on our culture and civilization. Songs convey the national anthems that inspire the pride of nations. We all may remember 150 members of Congress singing a chorus of "God Bless America" on the steps of the U.S. Capitol to show their solidarity after the barbaric attacks on the World Trade Center on September 11, 2001. Songs lift the battle cry that emboldens raiding armies. Songs (i.e., rap, rock and roll, hip hop, R&B, etc.) have created cultures and influenced entire generations. Do you remember hearing, reading about, or experiencing the musical effects of Woodstock, the Beatles, Run DMC, or Michael Jackson's *Thriller* album?

The classical music of the German composers (i.e., Handel's *Messiah,* Bach's *Magnificat,* Beethoven's *Ninth Symphony,* and Brahms' *Lullaby*) was used in the Holocaust to promote Hitler's Aryan superiority and as background music to lull the prisoners into submission and soothe the emotions of the Jews slated to die in the atrocious gas chambers. Music creates a mood and produces a sensory, emotional, and cognitive response in your brain that enhances learning and memory. A song can be a trigger to a deluge of good or bad memories and personal experiences. So it is no wonder that in today's culture, songs continue to captivate us and capture a dominant place in our secular and sacred society.

Songs are so powerful that they even have the capacity to increase blood flow! Visionary music educator and neuroscientist Eric Jensen writes, "With the advent of brain-imaging devices, we learned that music activates many places in the brain. We can also now see how music impacts blood flow. While alone this finding may not seem earth-shaking, it lays the foundation for the subsequent thesis that music making impacts memory, stress, and the immune system, all of which are dependent on blood flow."[1] Our God is an awesome wonder! He created us so that music will impact our blood! We know that life is in the blood (Gen. 9:4). So music *can* change our lives! This is why God placed song at the heart of humankind's expressions of praise. A song drenched in Holy Spirit power creates a pathway to spiritual conversion that will transfigure your life! However, without a clear knowledge and understanding of the power of music, it is our love of songs, not our longing for salvation that seems to dominate our praise and worship to God.

Throughout David's triumphs and tribulations, his songs were simply melodies that led him into a deeper, more intimate relationship with His Savior. David was *knowledgable*. He understood that his life was ordained and anointed by God. Even in adversity and the mayhem of his unpredictable escapades, David knew that music was the method he used to transcend his trials and lift him into God's protective love and majesty. Are we, like David, using our songs to deepen our intimate relationship with the Lord, or are our songs just shallow forms of praise to satisfy our religious urges? Is it your love of God that drives you to use your songs to draw close and feel the radiant light of His presence? Or is it the love of songs that has captured your heart and diverted your focus from God which may lead you into spiritual darkness?

Throughout David's numerous difficulties, the Bible writers continued to say he was wise and the Lord was with him (1 Sam. 18:14, 30). David was so wise that he knew he could not let his fugitive status dictate his spiritual condition. Whether he experienced a trial or a triumph, David's circumstances never altered his faith or focus on God. He understood that God is the King of kings and Lord of lords; He is worthy of praise (Ps. 69:30). He is the Good Shepherd who would never forsake His sheep. Even after he was crowned king of Israel,

> Praise is not predicated on how we feel or our circumstances. Praise is offered to God because God is God.

David remained a simple songwriter who gave God his whole heart, mind, and soul in praise.

In praise we humble ourselves before God and give him our lives. So when David finally became king of Israel after the untimely and vicious death of King Saul and his three sons, the practice of praise was the beat of his heart. Praise was the course of his life. Now at the age of thirty, David began his forty-year reign as king of Israel, intent on pleasing God. Yet despite his good intentions, David's coronation was marred by an infamous act of praise that had punitive results.

PRAISE PRACTICES

"So all the elders (tribal leaders) of Israel came to the king at Hebron, and King David made a covenant with them at Hebron before the Lord, and they anointed him king over Israel" (2 Sam. 5:3, AMP). David was anointed king three times in his life. First David was anointed as a young boy by Samuel (1 Sam. 16:13), second as king over the tribe of Judah (2 Sam. 2:4), and third as king of all Israel (2 Sam. 5:3). King David knew his kingdom had to be God-centered. Therefore his motives for bringing the ark of God to Jerusalem were both noble and wise. He intended to establish a united kingdom that housed a central place of worship. He also purposed to establish his seat of rulership and judicial power as a symbol of glory to the one true God. As a true worshiper, David understood the power of God's presence. Bringing the ark of God, which symbolized His presence (1 Sam. 4:4, 21), to Jerusalem would signify that God Himself lived amidst the Israelite nation.

So David proceeded with thirty-thousand choice men to transport the ark. Second Samuel 6:3 (AMP) reads, "And they set the ark of God upon a new cart and brought it out of the house of Abinadab, which was on the hill; and Uzzah and Ahio, sons of Abinadab, drove the new cart." What a praise production! David and the Israelite people believed that putting the ark of God on a new cart led by a retinue of thirty thousand dignitaries was the proper way to transport it. Unfortunately, in the decades that passed since the ark was in Israel's possession, they had forgotten the ark was designed by God to be carried only by the Levites (Exod. 25:14; Num. 4:15, 18). The ark was not supposed to be carried any other way. Not even the most modern-day, technical approach would be acceptable.

To David, transporting the ark on a new cart may have sounded like the quickest way to get the ark to Jerusalem and a fantastic, innovative, and forward-thinking idea. This was the high-tech method established decades earlier by the industrialized Philistines (1 Sam. 13:19–20) who had stolen the ark from Israel. But throughout the seven months it was in Philistine possession, God pronounced a plague of rats, tumors, and death in all of their cities. So naturally, the Philistines decided to return the ark. Smart move! Placing the ark on a new cart was the Philistines' earnest and desperate effort to rid themselves of the ark quickly, show repentance, and give glory to the foreign and powerful God of Israel. This was the way in which the pagan Philistines devised to give God a trespass offering and tried to cleanse their land of the plagues (1 Sam. 6:4–9). The Philistines filled the cart with an offering of golden rats and golden tumors. They did the best they could. They offered God the worldly worship practices they knew to perform. God accepted the ark from the Philistines because, unlike Israel, they did not know His laws. The heathen Philistines honored God by returning the ark the best way they knew how.

Why is it, then, that those of us who are in the church continue to imitate the world's secular praise practices? Are we creating a praise production just like King David by imitating the pagan practices of the nonbelievers around us? God gave Israel His Ten Commandments along with explicit worship instructions that the Philistines were not privileged to have (Exod. 20–31). The Israelites were held to the *highest* standard because they were given the requirements for praise and worship from God Himself. Yet despite this wealth of knowledge, the Israelites thought it would be better and more expedient to transport the ark using the modern methods of their idolatrous neighbors. They wanted to behave like the surrounding pagan nations and use a more cutting-edge, high-tech approach to praise. They did not want to practice ancient beliefs that were written by God and handed down by His Prophet Moses. They were looking for a fresh, new way to offer praise.

Are we doing the same thing today? Do we neglect God's laws, and then search the world for fresh, new ways to offer praise? The Ten Commandments outline methods for true worship which are a love relationship between God and man (Exod. 20; Matt. 22:37–40). God's Holy Word is our blueprint for giving praise. But even with this wealth of godly knowledge, are we instead using the world's methods to dictate our praise practices?

Many of today's praise songs and worship sets are patterned to meet the world's trendy secular music standards. Are we using the world's latest lyrics and beats to enter into the presence of God? Is our worship time with God more focused on the newest technology than theology? Are we using praise practices that are current but not consecrated? Do we mingle sacred sacraments with pagan practices and call it acceptable praise? Please do not misunderstand me. There is nothing wrong with using the latest technology or being culturally relevant in your praise music. The Bible instructs us to use relevant messages to reach the masses (Isa. 42:10; Ps. 40:3; Ps. 96:1). However, there is a problem with your worship when the production, rather than God's praise, is your primary focus. It is time to let our understanding of God's Word, and not the ways of the world, become our uncompromising standard to offer pure praise.

> Then David and all the house of Israel played music before the LORD on all kinds of instruments of fir wood, on harps, on stringed instruments, on tambourines, on sistrums, and on cymbals. And when they came to Nachon's threshing floor, Uzzah put out his hand to the ark of God and took hold of it, for the oxen stumbled. Then the anger of the LORD was

aroused against Uzzah, and God struck him there for his error; and he died there by the ark of God....David was afraid of the LORD that day; and he said, "How can the ark of the LORD come to me?"

—2 SAMUEL 6:5–9

Uzzah's death was devastating to David and the infantile nation of Israel. It remains a topic of debate and mystery to us even today. I have heard people say that the list of instruments played in the first failed attempt (2 Sam. 6:5) differs from the list of instruments played in the second successful attempt (1 Chron. 15:28) to bring the ark to Jerusalem. Therefore, the music and instruments were a factor in the worship that was unacceptable and ultimately resulted in Uzzah's death. The observation about the differing instruments in the first versus the second attempt is true. Let's take a closer look. See the chart below:

First Failed Attempt Ark brought to Obed-Edom (2 Sam. 6:5-9)	Second Successful Attempt Ark brought to Jerusalem (1 Chron. 15:27-28)
1. Instruments of Fir wood	1. Singers
2. Harps	2. Shouting
3. Stringed Instruments	3. Trumpets
4. Tambourines	4. Cymbals
5. Sistrums	5. Stringed Instruments
6. Cymbals	6. Harps

In the first failed attempt, all kinds of instruments of fir wood (or cedar trees), sistrums, and tambourines were played. The list of instruments changed in the second successful attempt. Neither instruments of fir wood, sistrums, nor tambourines were played in the second attempt. They were replaced with singers, trumpets, and people shouting. My goodness, trumpets and shouters? That kind of loud praise would not be allowed to happen in some of our churches today; it would be deemed inappropriate! Yet this vibrant, resounding praise was acceptable to God. I have heard people conclude that the first worship processional was unacceptable to God due to the improper instruments that were played. These were not the instruments prescribed for worship. However the Bible does *not* show support for that theory. The Prophet Samuel makes it clear that Uzzah's death had nothing to do with the instruments used. Scripture explains the reason for Uzzah's death: "God struck him there for his error" (2 Sam. 6:7). So what *was* Uzzah's error?

As a Levite, son of Abinadab, Uzzah knew he was not supposed to touch the ark. Only the sons of Aaron could touch the holy articles in the temple (Num. 4:4–15). Uzzah was raised by the Levite tribe who was tasked with being the caretakers of the temple and its furnishings. The Levites stood in the presence of Almighty God where His glory was revealed and must be reverenced. The tribe of Levi could only carry the temple furnishings once they had been covered by Aaron and his sons (Num. 4:15). When the Philistines returned the ark to Israel, the men of Kirjath Jearim brought the ark to Abinadab's home. It remained there in Uzzah's home for twenty years (1 Sam. 7:1–2). God gave the Levites explicit commands on how to minister before the ark (Num. 4:15–20). It was clear that if they were to touch the ark, they would die. Therefore Uzzah's death was solely a result of his presumption and rebellion against God.

In the book *Patriarchs and Prophets,* Ellen White agrees and explains:

> The fate of Uzzah was a divine judgement upon the violation of the most explicit command. Through Moses the Lord had given special instruction concerning the transportation of the ark. None but the priests, the descendants of Aaron, were to touch it, or even look upon it uncovered. The divine direction was, 'The sons of Kohath shall come to bear it: but they shall not touch any holy thing, lest they die' (Num. 4:15). The

priests were to cover the ark, and then the Kohathites must lift it by the staves, which were placed in the rings upon each side of the ark and never removed. To the Gershonites and Merarites, who had in charge the curtains and boards and pillars of the tabernacle, Moses gave carts and oxen for the transportation of that which was committed to them. "But unto the sons of Kohath he gave none: because the service of the sanctuary belonging unto them was that they should bear *upon their shoulders*" (Num. 7:9). Thus in the bringing of the ark from Kirjath Jearim, there had been a direct and inexcusable disregard of the Lord's direction.[2]

Today are we still making the same presumptuous, rebellious, and inexcusable error that Uzzah and the Israelites made? Are we quick to blame the instruments when our praise is chaotic or unsuccessful, instead of looking deep within our souls to determine whether our behavior follows the Lord's commands? The music that was used in the successful attempt to bring the ark to Jerusalem added a vocal dimension of singers, and shouters to the instrumentation that now included trumpets. The praise that was offered in the successful attempt was loud, expressive, and exuberant. It was both vocal and instrumental as God had prescribed (Exod. 15:1; Num. 10:8; Ps. 132:9). But when our praise is unacceptable, is it the volume and the choice of musical instruments that causes mayhem, or our own characters and behaviors that meddle with our offerings? Praise to God is about His love relationship with ordinary, sinful people who surrender their hearts and souls in worship, *not the music*! True praise is about the transformational power of God penetrating the life of the worshiper, *not the music* dictating the depths of your devotion.

To offer God the praise that He prescribes, we must follow His directions. We must be knowledgeable and obedient to God's Holy Word. Do we plan elaborate programs void of godly guidelines that kills our sacrifice of praise because our self-proclaimed methods are unsuitable? Why are we content to be expert musicians yet novice Bible students? How can we instill deep change in our praise practices so that God will be glorified? David's second attempt to bring the ark to Jerusalem was successful because he realized his error. The ark could not be carried or handled by ordinary people in an ordinary fashion. In First Chronicles 15:2, we read, "Then David said, 'No one may carry the ark of God but the Levites, for the LORD has chosen them to carry the ark of God and to minister before Him forever.'" David acknowledged his mistake as a king and carefully and purposefully enacted a divine plan to remedy the problem and reinstate the music ministry of the Levites.

LEVITE LESSONS

1. Although God uses ordinary people, being an artist for God is no ordinary task.

2. Our worship will venture deep into the hearts of men when it is overflowing with the Word of God.

3. A song bathed in Holy Spirit power creates a pathway to spiritual conversion that will transfigure your life!

4. Praise is not predicated on how we feel or on our circumstances. Praise is offered to God because God is God.

5. God's Holy Word is our blueprint for giving praise.

6. True praise is about the transformational power of God penetrating the life of the worshiper, *not the music* dictating the depths of your devotion.

7. To offer God the praise that He prescribes, we must follow His directions. We must be knowledgeable and obedient to God's Holy Word.

PRACTICAL PRAISE QUESTIONS

What steps can you take to avoid behaving like the Israelites who did not follow God's commands for giving praise?

How can you refrain from blaming the instruments for the church's musical mayhem and instead begin to examine your own heart before God?

ENDNOTES

1.   Eric Jensen, *Music with the Brain in Mind* (Thousand Oaks, CA: Corwin Press, 2000), 14.

2.   Ellen G. White, *Patriarchs and Prophets* (Mountain View, CA: Pacific Press, 1958), 705.

Chapter 4

RUNNING BACK TO YOU

The Lord is my shepherd; I shall not want.

—PSALM 23:1

SONGS OF PRAISE

ALTHOUGH DAVID EXPERIENCED numerous trage-dies and triumphs in his life, he was never deterred from giving God the highest praise. As a celebrated writer, David composed melodies as a testament to his lifelong devotion to God. Despite David's remarkable stature as an Israelite king, most scholars and theologians would agree that his most notable legacy was the Book of Psalms. Undoubtedly, Psalms is the most frequently quoted book of the Bible. Amongst the Psalms, the twenty-third psalm towers above the rest as the most familiar and beloved. While in battle, David composed the twenty-third psalm with calm assurance. He wrote, "The Lord is my shepherd; I shall not want." This psalm offers to us a divine guarantee that we will lack nothing. It asserts there is nothing we need that we will be without.

Professor Patrick Miller, a theologian at Princeton Theological Seminary, states,

> The corollary of knowing God as one's shepherd is given in the following sentences; "I shall not want," or "I do not lack." The absolute use of the verb *hāsar* "to want, lack"—that is, the verb used without any object such as food, help, or just anything—is unusual. Indeed it occurs only one other time, in Neh. 9:21 in reference to Israel's experience of God's care

in the wilderness. "Forty years you sustained them in the wilderness and they did not lack."....The claim, "I do not lack" is comprehensive, all-inclusive. With the Lord as shepherd, nothing is lacking for life.[1]

What a divine promise! With the Lord as our shepherd, we will have *everything we need*. We will lack absolutely nothing! So then, why do most of us believe that the Bible lacks clear, modern instructions on musical praise? Since God is the Creator and source of everything, why do we find ourselves without godly instructions for our music? Why are we as Bible-believing Christians embattled by worship wars or trapped in the wilderness of worship-style strife? I say that, like David, we must declare in the worship battle, "The Lord is my shepherd, I shall not want"!

Have you noticed that when most worship leaders search for music resources, it is rare that principles from the Bible are offered or mentioned? It seems that our praise is not dependent on the Word of God. Why have we wandered so far away from using the Bible as our praise blueprint? I believe the culprit is a lack of biblical knowledge and understanding. We rely on secular standards for spiritual solutions, even when these insufficient methods create a void deep in our souls. There is no matter in heaven or on Earth in which God will leave us thirsting for the truth. God's Word is truth (John 17:17). In His discussion with the woman at the well regarding worship, Jesus gave us this guarantee: "But those who drink the water I give will never be thirsty again. It becomes a fresh, bubbling spring within them, giving them eternal life" (John 4:14, NLT)." So, let's run back to the Bible and drink from God's Holy Word so that He can infuse our praise with the power of eternal life!

To begin our journey back to the Bible, first we must stop looking on the surface. We should thoroughly search the Scriptures to uncover the secrets of song and the mystery of music. We should look at concepts that may be buried in the Bible to determine if they offer any guidelines for musical praise. God has promised to reveal the deep things out of darkness (Job 12:22). David understood that God's Word is a lamp to our feet and a light to our path (Ps. 119:105). So why does it seem like we are drowning in the dark depths of worship discord while the life-saving reserves of praise just float by unnoticed and unheard? Since it is in the Book of Psalms that David assures us we will not want, then I believe that what we *want* ought to be found within its pages! So let's explore together and see what we discover.

The Book of Psalms contains one of the greatest collections of songs, prayers, and poetry that spans one thousand years from the time of Moses to the time of the return of the Israelite exiles from Babylonian captivity. The Psalms were written by ordinary men under the supernatural inspiration of the Holy Spirit. In fact, the Psalms writers are named in over two-thirds of its 150 chapters! The writers include Moses (Ps. 90), King David (over 75 psalms total), and Solomon (Ps. 72; 127). There are also over twenty psalms that were written by Levites whom David had put in charge of the music in the temple (1 Chron. 6:31–48; 15:16–17). These writers include Asaph (Ps. 50, 73–83); Heman (Ps. 88); Ethan (Ps. 89); and the sons of Korah (Ps. 42, 44–49, 84–85, 87).

In his book *Interpreting the Psalms,* Mark Futato tells us the purpose of the psalms. Futato shares,

> While many of the psalms were originally composed for use in public worship, it cannot be demonstrated that all were. In addition, the function of a given psalm in its original context and the function of that same psalm in the context of the completed Book of Psalms are not necessarily the same. For example, many psalms were originally human words to God in prayer and praise. But once included in the canonical book, these texts became God's word to humans to teach us how to pray and praise."[2]

God bestows upon song such a prominent and permanent place in salvation history that He nestled a hymnal that can be used as a handbook in His Holy Word! Perhaps analyzing music from the pages of the psalms can deepen our understanding and reveal some biblical principles for selecting and composing proper praise music today.

The Psalms is God's word to us to teach us how to pray and praise. Wow, isn't that marvelous! Therefore, the Book of Psalms is God's holy hymnal.

Psalms is divided into five books: Book I: 1–41; Book II: 42–72; Book III: 73–89; Book IV: 90–106; Book V: 107–150. These divisions have both a spiritual and traditional interpretation. In Scripture, the number five symbolizes God's grace. The spiritual symbol of God's grace—unmerited favor—associated with the number five can be seen repeatedly throughout Scripture. There were five Levitical offerings (Lev. 1–5); David collected five smooth stones to fight and kill Goliath (1 Sam. 17:40); Jesus multiplied five loaves to feed the five thousand (Matt. 14:17); and the woman at the well had five husbands (John 4:18). Each time the number five is used in Scripture it signifies that God is about to bestow a full measure of His grace. The five books of Psalms is a melodious memorial of God's grace to His people.

The traditional interpretation of the five books of Psalms is evidenced by David's connection to Moses. (Note: There is another significant connection between David and Moses in the book *Levite Praise* on page 123.) Futato explains, "As Moses gave five books of laws to Israel, so David gave five books of Psalms to Israel . . . the book of Psalms is in five sections because the five books of the Psalms are just like the five books of Moses: the five books of the Psalms are fundamentally 'instruction' to be meditated on."[3] Psalms is not just a book of songs. Psalms was given by God as a holy inheritance—a legacy of traditions and instructions to be meditated on, and then passed down and applied through the ages. Therefore in the Psalms, we are able to receive God's grace to understand the spiritual significance of praise through examining its traditions. For this reason, our praise songs should contain both traditions and instructions that we pass down to future generations.

Let's look to see what lessons we can find buried in the songs of the Psalms. Chances are we might clearly identify some timeless worship principles by analyzing the Psalms' structure.

THE STRUCTURE OF PRAISE

Futato identifies six subcategories into which the Psalms can be subdivided:

1. **Hymns**: Songs that celebrate God as Creator and Redeemer. Hymns invite all to the concert of praise (Ps. 29; 47; 103; 117; 118; etc.).

2. **Laments:** Songs of disorientation that give us permission to let the tears flow in times when we may feel perplexed, forsaken, fearful, overwhelmed, angry, lost, or in despair (Ps. 6; 22; 30; 44; 88; etc.).

3. **Songs of thanksgiving:** Songs that express joy and gratitude to God for his deliverance (Ps. 34; 40; 75; 116; 144; etc.).

4. **Songs of confidence:** Songs of unwavering confidence or trust in God's ability and willingness to deliver us from adverse circumstances (Ps. 16; 23; 27; 62; 91; etc.).

5. **Divine kingship songs:** Songs that focus on the kingship of God (Ps. 93; 95; 96; 97; 99; etc.).

6. **Wisdom songs:** Songs that teach us how to put God's instructions into practice in many of the major areas of life (Ps. 19; 37; 49; 73; 112; etc.).

HYMNS

The first observation that we can easily make from these six subcategories is that not all psalms are hymns. The hymns are songs that celebrate God for His creative and redemptive powers. These songs bring us into a concert of praise to extol the restorative creatorship that only a Sovereign God can possess. For example, in Psalm 29:1–4, David declares, "Give unto the LORD, O you mighty ones. Give unto the LORD glory and strength. Give unto the LORD the glory due His name; worship the LORD in the beauty of holiness. The voice of the LORD is over the waters; the God of glory thunders; the LORD is over many waters. The voice of the LORD is powerful; the voice of the LORD is full of majesty." In Ps. 47:1–2, the sons of Korah exclaim, "Oh, clap your hands, all you peoples! Shout to God with the voice of triumph. For the LORD Most High is awesome, He is a great King over all the earth." David proclaimed, "Bless the LORD, O my soul; and all that is within me bless His holy name! Bless the LORD, O my soul, and forget not all His benefits: who forgives all your iniquities, who heals all your diseases, who redeems your life from destruction" (Ps. 103:1–4). Can't you see the vivid images of our Mighty Creator, Redeemer God in these glorious hymns?

Although all of the psalms contain spiritual instructions that were used for public worship, not all psalms were written exclusively for temple worship. In fact, the temple itself was not designed by David for the practice of corporate worship. *The IVP Bible Background Commentary* confirms,

> The temple was not a structure designed for corporate worship. It was a structure to provide a place for God to dwell in the midst of his people. It had to be maintained in holiness and purity so that God's continuing presence could be vouchsafed. The priests existed to maintain that purity and to control access. The temple idea was not invented so that there would be a place to offer sacrifices. Rather, several of the

sacrifices existed as a means of maintaining the temple. God's presence was the most important element to preserve.[4]

The Prophet Samuel concurs with this notion that the temple was a place for God to dwell in his account of David's motives for erecting God's house. Second Samuel 7:1–2 reads, "Now it came to pass when the king was dwelling in his house, and the LORD had given him rest from all his enemies all around, that the king said to Nathan the prophet, 'See now, I dwell in a house of cedar, but the ark of God dwells inside tent curtains.'" David's deepest desire in constructing the temple was to design a place for God's presence to dwell among his people. Solomon understood and carried out his father David's wishes. At the completion of the temple—when the ark was brought into its place in the inner sanctuary—Solomon said, "The LORD said He would dwell in the dark cloud. I have surely built You an exalted house, and a place for You to dwell in forever" (2 Chron. 6:1–2). So as we sing our hymns of praise, each selection should create an atmosphere that allows God's presence to dwell in His temple which is within us (1 Cor. 6:19).

In her book *Jesus Today,* Sarah Young explains this magnificent mystery of God dwelling within us.

> You are in Me and I am in you. This is a profound mystery. I am the infinite Creator and Sustainer of the entire universe. You are a finite, fallen human being. Yet you and I live not just *with* each other but also *in* each other. You are filled with My *divine Presence.* This is a deeper, fuller union than you can find in any human relationship. Even people who have been married many decades cannot know all the thoughts and feelings of their spouse. But I know *everything* about you—from your deepest thoughts and feelings to the events you will encounter tomorrow.[5]

LAMENTS, SONGS OF THANKSGIVING, AND SONGS OF CONFIDENCE

The next three subcategories (laments, songs of thanksgiving, and songs of confidence) are for our private times in life when we need to hear from the Lord. Lament songs are particularly fascinating. They are songs of disorientation composed in our confidential times of deep sorrow, grief, and pain. In his text *Ancient Psalms and Modern Worship,* Edward Curtis explains,

> Laments outnumber every other kind of psalm in the Psalter; almost a third of the psalms belong to this category. Laments have their origin in situations of distress from which the psalmists cried out to God for help and deliverance. These psalms follow a generally similar form, though they stem from a wide variety of specific situations. Sometimes they reflect community concerns; sometimes they are the cries of individuals. They reflect a wide assortment of troubles—political pressure, physical illness, loneliness, oppression, and a variety of spiritual needs. Interestingly, every lament includes an element of praise.[6]

In Psalm 22:1–3, David illustrates this pattern of movement from pain and praise: "My God, My God, why have You forsaken Me? Why are You so far from helping Me, and from the words of My groaning? O My God, I cry in the daytime, but You do not hear; and in the night season, and am not silent. But You are holy, enthroned in the praises of Israel." Lament songs are critical for the Christian life. They give us an appropriate outlet for the myriad of woes we face. In these songs we can express all our tribulations. No problem is too sacred or too secular to confess to Jesus Christ. Accordingly, the psalms teach us how to truly cry out to God in our pain. When we lift our songs of despair to God yet learn to delight in His presence, even our pain will be peppered with genuine praise!

I must admit, it is not easy to move from a painful trial to earnest praise. Many times we as worship leaders become spiritually weak when we encounter a personal crisis. I know on December 6, 2006, when my sister was diagnosed with Stage IV breast cancer, our family was devastated and wracked with pain. During the seven months that followed, my sister fought valiantly to live. It was heartrending when she lost her battle with cancer on June 9, 2007. During this crucible, it was hard to fathom giving God praise. Yet through it all, I praised Him anyhow! I praised Him when I couldn't breathe because of the crushing heartbreak. I trusted God in the midst of my raging storm. So this is when the techniques that we use in song preparation can take on a new meaning.

This is why it is essential to understand the power and process of lamentation. We can go to God with our deepest sorrows and burden Him with our grief. Jesus Christ will bear our burdens. As we rely on Him and dwell in His presence, eventually our

> I learned that in the same way we rehearse music until we are proficient, we can practice giving God praise in the midst of our trials until we are at peace.

load, no matter how heavy, will become light (Matt. 11:29–30).

The categories of thanksgiving and confidence offer poignant songs as well. These are songs of joy and gratitude for God's provision and deliverance. These songs illustrate trust and unswerving confidence in times of adversity or desperate uncertainty.

Psalm 34 attests to David's confidence in God for deliverance when he pretended to be insane so he could escape Abimelech (a title used by many Philistine kings). He sang, "I will bless the Lord at all times; His praise shall continually be in my mouth. My soul shall make its boast in the LORD; the humble shall hear of it and be glad. Oh, magnify the LORD with me, and let us exalt His name together" (Ps. 34:1–3). Psalm 34 proves that we can always give God joyous praise for His promise of protection and deliverance even in times of total insanity!

The songs contained in the Psalms allow God to govern our every emotion. This is essential to comprehend. Typically, artists and musicians allow circumstances to dictate their passions and feelings. Wouldn't you agree? However, joy, happiness, contentment, sadness, anger, grief, frustration, despair, and fear can all be expressed to God in faith. Through song, we can declare our trust in God even in times of turmoil. In Psalm 27:1–3, David offers us an exuberant declaration of his faith: "The LORD is my light and my salvation; whom shall I fear? The LORD is the strength of my life; of whom shall I be afraid? When the wicked came against me to eat up my flesh, my enemies and foes, they stumbled and fell. Though an army may encamp against me, my heart shall not fear; though war may rise against me, in this I *will be* confident." Ps. 18:30 says, "*As for* God, His way *is* perfect; the word of the LORD is proven; He is a shield to all who trust in Him." What a testament of complete faith and confidence in God in the face of fear! Through the Word of the Lord written in the songs of the Psalms, we can all exclaim in our worst tragedies, "God is my Protector and Redeemer; in Him alone will I put my trust!"

The songs of praise in the Psalms provide us with invaluable lessons. God is always there when we need Him. Whether our experiences are triumphant or tragic, God still inhabits our praise (Ps. 22:3). It is in your times of despair that you must prove God's powerful presence in your life. There is a practical application woven into the Psalms that can be evidenced in the songs of lament, confidence, and thanksgiving. We can develop a spiritual bond through musical praise as we beseech God in diverse situations. When we are happy, sad, thankful, contented, confident, or need advice, God's Word will supply our solutions and salvation. The Psalms were songs written as personal petitions for God's presence to dwell among us. But *first*, we need God's presence to dwell within us. For that to happen, He must be invited into our hearts and minds. Despite our circumstances, our songs of praise should lead us to connect to the heart of God.

So as you write or select your praise songs, the Book of Psalms can be your guide. Even though we typically write praise songs for use in our worship services, Psalms clearly illustrates that not all praise songs were written for church use. *But we must be clear on which songs are suitable for a sacred versus a secular venue.* Praise songs that may not be conducive for a sacred sanctuary service can still serve a spiritual and ennobling purpose in our secular lives. There are times that we all have experienced songs being played in church that are inappropriate for the worship service. We can all admit that there are numerous Christian songs that we would deem unsuitable for the sanctuary.

However this does not mean these songs *do not* serve a higher purpose. Some of these songs are best suited for entertainment in our secular lives. These songs can be appropriate for fellowship, fun, or casual day-to-day activities. Events like a social gathering, a concert, a Christian café, a workout, jogging, a long walk, driving in your car, working on the job, relaxing or doing chores at home, etc., would benefit from these songs. I am sure you could think of many more activities to add to your own list. Yet despite their usage outside the sanctuary or divine worship service, these melodies still serve a spiritual and noble purpose. These tunes can create a soundtrack throughout your day to uplift, encourage, console, energize, and inspire you while still directing your heart and mind to extol and recognize the presence of God.

Worship is a lifestyle.

It does not only happen in church on Sabbath. Therefore, we can conclude that the psalms were used in a lifestyle of worship. This lifestyle of worship glorified God's presence during secular and sacred, private and public expressions of praise.

DIVINE KINGSHIP AND WISDOM SONGS

The final two categories, the divine kingship and wisdom songs, also serve a vital purpose. The divine kingship songs demonstrate God's rulership. These songs reflect our acknowledgement of the sovereignty and omnipotence of God in our lives and on the Earth.

These unique praise songs constantly remind us to humbly relinquish our human authority to God's divine majesty. These songs remind us that God is sovereign.

Singers and musicians can certainly benefit from this reminder. Many times, we tend to set up little kingdoms here on Earth where we think in our giftedness we reign supreme! Everything we do centers around me, myself, and I. At times, even the songs we select for worship are based solely on our self-centered personal preferences. Typically we select only the songs we know, love, consider most current, have practiced, and find personally appealing. In contrast, we seldom select songs that consider the spiritual needs of our congregations. This regular self-centeredness is openly praised in our individualistic culture. We even see the effects of this self-absorbed mindset in one of the world's most powerful brands and largest technology providers: Apple Inc. Their product names tell it all. We use the iPhone, iPod, iPad, and iMac all accessible at me.com. Every product begins with "I" and centers on "me." Truthfully, you can't get more self-centered than that!

So the divine kingship psalms help to restore the proper order between God and man: "Oh come, let us sing to the LORD! Let us shout joyfully to the Rock of our salvation. Let us come before His presence with thanksgiving; let us shout joyfully to Him with psalms. For the LORD is the great God, and the great King above all gods" (Ps. 95:1–3). In our praise, God is paramount. So the Book of Psalms provides us with a pathway to proper musical praise. If we follow these instructions, every song, note, and lyric would impress our minds to run back to our Lord and King, Jesus Christ.

APPROPRIATE PRAISE

Once the new Israelite nation settled in Jerusalem, David erected a tent-like tabernacle for the ark of God. At last, transporting the ark to its resting place would be a joyous and festive occasion. After the offerings of sacrifice, King David gave a public blessing and distributed the gracious gift of free food to everyone throughout the land (1 Chron. 16:2–3). Then he appointed some of the Levites to minister before the ark daily. Asaph and his brothers were stationed in rank to commemorate, thank, and praise God in an orderly fashion. They were assigned to play stringed instruments and harps, to make music with the cymbals, and to blow the trumpets before the ark (1 Chron. 16:4–6). The management of this majestic music was prescribed by God for the tabernacle service.

It was on this momentous day, that David delivered a thanksgiving psalm to his music minister, Asaph. This psalm was no ordinary song. This psalm was a song of praise that revealed to the Israelites the purpose and practice of God-honoring worship. It revealed the recipe for a reverent response to God. Zinke agrees with this observation: "According to 1 Chronicles 16:7, David presented to Asaph his chief musician, a new song of thanksgiving and praise on the day that the ark was moved to Jerusalem. This praise psalm consists of two important aspects of worship; the revelation of God as One worthy of worship and the appropriate response of the worshiper."[7] Let's examine the components of appropriate praise and worship together:

> Oh, *give thanks* to the LORD!
>> *Call* upon His name;
> *Make known* His deeds among the peoples!
>> *Sing* to Him, *sing psalms* to Him;
>> *Talk* of all His wondrous works!
> *Glory* in His holy name;
>> Let the hearts of those *rejoice* who *seek* the LORD!
> *Seek* the LORD and His strength;
>> *Seek* His face evermore!
> *Remember* His marvelous works which He has done,
>> His wonders, and the *judgments* of His mouth,
> O seed of Israel His *servant*,
>> You children of Jacob, His *chosen* ones!
>> —1 Chronicles 16:8–13; Psalm 105:1–6

The first key observation is that genuine worship is active *not* passive. This psalm is brimming with action words. These action words paint a vivid picture of our praise to God. A clear understanding of the Hebrew terms unwraps the verses' true meaning. First, we must *give thanks* to the LORD. Here David teaches us that genuine worship flows from a thankful heart. The Hebrew word used for *give thanks* not only means to praise, but to make confession. We should first confess our sins in order to confess our praise and thankfulness to God. To *call* on the Lord means to call, recite, read, and proclaim. It is our ability to call on the name of the Lord in our music and praise that provides power! Many Christian songwriters aim to write crossover music that does not proclaim the name of Jesus. They do this to achieve popularity and fame. However, David instructs us to compose songs that call on and proclaim the name of Jesus because these songs will have Holy Spirit inspiration and powerful spiritual influence.

We can *make known* God's deeds in our lives. Each one of us can become a living testimony by sharing the goodness of God. Our family, friends, neighbors, and community will praise God by seeing the manifestation of His love and grace through us. We can share God's divine deeds with others through a lifestyle of worship and personal testimony. The word *sing* is repeated twice by David to emphasize the manner in which we can appropriately sing to God. The first time *sing* is used it refers to *singers* and *songstresses*. This righteous reference includes the singing of men and women! In his magnificent composition, David acknowledges that both males and females are chosen to sing God's praise (Neh. 7:67). Then, *sing psalms to Him* indicates that both vocal music and instrumental music are prescribed to sing God's praise. The term *talk* means to meditate, muse, commune, and even complain to God. This talking, testifying, singing, and faithful fretting is a manner of communication that exalts God's majesty despite our daily disappointments, mysteries in life, and mayhem of this world.

To *glory* means to shine, to flash forth light, to praise, and to boast. Here is where musicians and church members may become confused. As musicians, we often feel the glory of God shine through us as we play our instruments or sing our songs. However, sometimes the more we are complimented by the members about our gifts, the more we begin to believe this glory is based on our own talents. God graciously allows us to share in the light of His glory when we offer Him genuine praise. However, this luminous, star-studded experience where God's brilliance is manifested through us has the sole purpose of leading people to Jesus Christ. It is not for the purpose of making music moguls! In the light of God's love, worship leaders are ministering servants, not superstars. In the light of God's love, worshipers become participants not spectators. The church should not be filled with an audience of fans but adoring followers who become ambassadors for Jesus Christ. In this dazzling worship atmosphere, we boast of Jesus Christ alone. Jesus is the Root and Offspring of David, the Bright and Morning Star (Rev. 22:16). We must remember and recognize there are no other stars in God's presence. In worship, Jesus Christ is the only Superstar! Then, we can *rejoice* and be glad with abandon because the Lord's holy name has been glorified.

The word *seek* has unique prominence in this passage. It is the only action word used three times. This repetition indicates that in appropriate praise our principle desire is to seek God in our worship. The number three symbolizes that the Trinity (Godhead) is active. We see this symbolism throughout Scripture, but it is most consistently demonstrated in the life of Jesus Christ. Jesus' ministry began at age 30, and it lasted for three-and-a-half years (Luke 3:23). He had three disciples who were closest to Him: Peter, James, and John (Matt. 17:1). He died at 33 years old with three Marys who attended Him at the cross (John 19:25). There were three crosses at Calvary (John 19:18). He died in the ninth hour (3 x 3 or 3 o'clock; Matt. 27:46) and rose on the third day (Matt. 27:62–63; 28:5–6)! In Scripture, the number three is powerful. When we actively seek God in our praise, His power is promised!

The three Hebrew terms used for *seek* have profound definitions. The first word for *seek* mean to seek, require, desire, exact, and request. In our seeking, we must understand what God requires and desires of us through our praise. In our worship we request to know God's exact will for our lives. In the Bible lexicon, the Syriac terminology for the word *seek* finds its primary powers by touching and feeling. Our praise has the power to touch the heart of God and enable us to feel His presence. The second word for *seek* means to resort to, frequent, consult, seek with care, follow with application. This word demonstrates that in order to maintain our praise purpose and power, we must seek the Lord with care. It requires resorting to frequent times of praise and worship—not just worship when we are in church. These times are not based only on our personal desires but what God requires from us—perpetual praise. This access to praise power—strength from God—comes by constant consultation. We go to God for His strength for everything in our lives. Then, we become followers of His Holy Word who are deeply devoted and obedient to His will.

In essence, when we think of the word *seek,* it should remind us that we come to worship to seek the King. Yet, our challenge with this method of seeking is that it is contrary to our modern Christian culture. Our brand of seeking is meager and self-centered. Instead of coming to *seek* the Lord in praise and give Him our all, we have come to *see.* We ignore the "k" which I believe should symbolize the King of kings. In worship we should come to seek the King! Yet many times, God is not central in our praise. Sadly, some of us have become spectators who come to church to *see* if the praise team is singing our style of music. Others of us are the audience who come to church to *see* if the pastor is preaching on a topic that we like. Then some of us are in the crowd who come to church to *see* our friends and fellowship with our fans. We have not come with a desperate desire to *seek* the King.

The third and final word for *seek* means to find, secure, to seek the face, to ask, request and to be sought. In this spiritual seeking, we not only desire to find God but to be fully immersed in His presence. We want to see His face! David understood the unique boldness of this request. It was clear to the Israelites that no one could see the face of God and live (Exod. 33:20). However, in this personal praise psalm seeking God's face is a command and the reward for our praise. In true praise, we will be in Jesus' presence forevermore. This reward is not only for our own asking and seeking, but because God Himself sought us by sending His Son, Jesus Christ to die for our sins. God's redemption promise is revealed in our earnest praise.

So God knows the frailty of our humanity, and in this psalm He uses David to call us to *remember* what He has done for us. Remember your Red Sea experiences and talk about the miracles in your life often. This will remind you that God is great and He can work awesome miracles in your life. This word for *remember* symbolizes a covenant. It is the same word used when God made His covenants with Noah, Abraham, and Moses, and when He wrote the Ten Commandments (Gen. 8:1; 19:29; Exod. 13:3; 20:8). In our praise, God promises to deliver us. In worship, God alone is the Judge. It is the *judgments* of His mouth, God's Holy Word, that should govern what is appropriate praise and not our own judgments or personal preferences. In true biblical praise to God we become the elect. We are His *servants*, and His *chosen* ones.

LEVITE LESSONS

1. With the Lord as our shepherd, we will have *everything we need*. We will lack absolutely nothing!

2. The Book of Psalms is God's word to us to teach us how to pray and praise.

3. Although all of the psalms contain spiritual instructions that were used for public worship, not all psalms were written exclusively for temple worship.

4. Our praise songs should contain both *traditions* and *instructions* that we passed down to future generations.

5. The songs contained in the Psalms allow God to govern our every emotion.

6. The Book of Psalms was used in a lifestyle of worship that glorified God's presence during secular and sacred, private and public expressions of praise.

7. In the light of God's love, worshipers become participants not spectators.

PRACTICAL PRAISE QUESTION

Does the music you listen to direct your thoughts toward or away from God?

ENDNOTES

1.   Patrick D. Miller, *Interpreting the Psalms* (Philadelphia: Fortress Press, 1986), 113–114.

2.   Mark D. Futato, David M. Howard Jr., eds., *Interpreting the Psalms: An Exegetical Handbook* (Grand Rapids: Kregel, 2007), 59.

3.   Ibid., 63.

4.   John H. Walton, Victor H. Matthews, and Mark W. Chavalas, *The IVP Bible Background Commentary Old Testament* (Downers Grove, IL: InterVarsity Press, 2000), 513.

5.   Sarah Young, *Jesus Today: Experiencing Hope Through His Presence* (Nashville, TN: Thomas Nelson, 2012), 66.

6.   Edward M. Curtis, *Ancient Psalms and Modern Worship*. Evangelical Theological Society Papers, 1992.

7.   Rosalie Zinke, *Worship* (Nampa, ID: Pacific Press, 2011), 49.

PART II:

Reveal

Chapter 5

INTO MY HEART

Then Nathan said to the king, "Go, do all that is
in your heart, for the LORD is with you."

—2 SAMUEL 7:3

PURPOSEFUL PRAISE

*T*HE PROPHET NATHAN smiled as he rested his head on his bed. He was contemplating the sweet peace that currently surrounded the fledgling kingdom of Israel. Finally, the Israelite nation was no longer at war with its enemies. Nathan had witnessed the ark of God brought with pageantry to its royal resting place in Jerusalem. It was a wonderful sight, and both he and David marveled at the glory of God and His goodness. The kingdom of Israel had been established by God with majesty, pomp, and power. David's newly constructed house of cedar represented the strength that the Israelite kingdom held. Yet right away, David fastened his heart and mind to undertake another unimaginable enterprise. He purposed in his heart to build a house for God. Nathan was pleased at the prospect and encouraged David to follow his heart. Tonight, Nathan lay on his bed thinking and dreaming of the magnificent results.

But his peaceful sleep was short-lived; as in times past, Nathan heard a familiar voice. Suddenly, he heard the voice of God. God's response to David's proposition was one of promise. Although God questioned the purpose of a house built for an infinite Jehovah to dwell in, He recognized David's aspiration to act in true adoration. So God sent a magnanimous message through Nathan. God promised to set up a dwelling place for the Israelites and established a royal dynasty for David and his descendants. The house that David would build for God's name would be accepted and rewarded through an everlasting throne and kingdom (2 Sam. 7:10–16).

When David heard these words from Nathan, he was overwhelmed. He was humbled by the bountiful gift and blessings God had bestowed on him. David immediately responded in prayer (2 Sam. 7:27). To show his gratitude, David spent time in God's presence in private praise. David "went in and sat before the Lord" (2 Sam. 7:18). Many times God gives us gifts that are immeasurable. As an artist, your talent is a tremendous gift from God. Do you *go in* and sit before the Lord in private to thank and honor Him for your gift? Or do you *go out* in public to promote yourself to others for adoration and acclaim? Private time in praise to God is paramount. But more importantly, submission to God's authority is the key to ministry success. By giving humble praise, David demonstrated his devotion to God in response to His blessing. Sovereign God ordained David's kingship and the Israelite kingdom with eternal meaning and purpose.

Many times the largest extent of our praise is only what we offer God in public. Most of us don't spend enough private time with God meditating on His works and His Word. Private time in praise to God is essential for proper spiritual nourishment. David tells us in Psalm 34:8, "O, taste and see that the LORD is good." Our pure praise is like a delicious meal that nourishes our souls. So what happens when we don't spend enough private time with God? Let's think of it like this. We all love to eat, right? Well, some of us more than others. However, whether you are a food fanatic or have an ordinary appetite, eating is vital to our mental and physical growth. In order to be healthy, we must eat daily. If we don't follow these dietary rules, our bodies will become diseased. What would happen if you were only allowed to eat one time per week? I believe that if you only ate once per week, when meal time came around, you would be starving. When you arrive at your weekly potluck and the food is served, it is unlikely that you would be cheerful, greet others, and spend time talking with people about their personal needs. You probably won't have a desire to socialize because you are starving. Your sole purpose would be to first feed yourself! I imagine you would squeeze through the crowd, fill your plate to overflowing, and then sit contented and inactive with your belly full.

Sadly, many of us act the same way with our one-day-per-week praise. We are spiritually starved and arrive at church ravenous because our daily worship is weak or nonexistent. When we enter into the banquet—God's House—spiritually starved, we focus on what is here for me instead of who is here for the Master. Unfortunately, because we are nearly empty, we fill up on the junk food of a bloated praise experience. Without proper spiritual nourishment, we can't focus on sharing our faith or impacting others with our worship. We can't give to others because we are too busy feeding ourselves. Yet we are starving for proper spiritual nourishment. We become bloated worshipers who are content with being full, instead of feeding others by sharing the Gospel of Jesus Christ. Spiritual starvation causes soul disease. We must digest God's Word daily and spend time in private praise so that others can taste and see the bounty of God's goodness in our lives.

God honored David's good intentions by blessing him and his descendants. However, David was not the one God ordained to build his temple. David lived a violent life. Because of this, God would not allow him to build the temple (1 Chron. 28:3). God had other plans. David's son Solomon would build his temple. Nevertheless, God recognized the goodness that was in David's heart and honored him for it (1 Kings 8:17–18). God had another purpose for David. Because of his love and transcendent trust in God's goodness, David did not gripe at this decision. On the contrary, he employed his administrative skills. He humbled himself and prepared the plans for the temple's construction! What a lesson for us to learn on how to be obedient, humble, and purposeful when disappointments come. David was not allowed to build the temple because of his past.

I can imagine that although God pronounced a blessing on David, this was a considerable disappointment. Building the temple was his big idea, and both he and Nathan thought this would please the Lord. Yet David's response to God's revelation was unprecedented. Instead of responding in resentment or anger, he became active. David decided to use his talents to help build God's temple in another purposeful way. Do you have goals you want to accomplish that God will not allow because of your past? Would you have the desire to build someone else's ministry when you believe that ministry should be yours? Some of us are building ministries that God has not ordained for us to build. As spiritual Levites, we are called to serve our pastors (Num. 3:5–6). Are you building your own kingdom by erecting a fortress of fame? Do you become resentful, envious, or even hypercritical when someone else is successful in a ministry that you feel should be yours?

Our sole purpose as music ministers
is to lift up Jesus Christ.

We do this by creating a sermon in song that will draw people into God's presence. Despite David's disappointment, he never lost sight of his purpose—to glorify God with his life of leadership. David determined in his heart to serve God with his gifts. He was wise and humble enough to also trust God to determine how and for what purpose his gifts would be used. What a lesson for us to learn today!

David was multi-talented. Yet God called him to accomplish a specific mission. David was a gifted songwriter. He was a prophet (Acts 2:29–30); priest (2 Sam. 6:14–18); and king (2 Sam. 2:4; 5:1–3). He was not a temple builder! So instead of being stymied, David turned his sights toward becoming a good king and one of the most prolific composers of the Bible. He did not sulk because he would not have the fame of being the first temple architect. Instead

David followed God by faith. King David became a *musicianary*. I first heard this term over a decade ago as I was working to complete my Master of Arts degree in Practical Theology, Worship, and Renewal at Regent University. Then it was used by Dr. Roberta King, Associate Professor of Communications and Ethnomusicology at Fuller Theological Seminary. She used it to adequately describe the unique calling of Christian musicians to the world. A musicianary uses the tool of music to spread the Gospel of Jesus Christ. A musicianary is a person who is devoted to the task of using music to attempt to persuade and convert others. David wrote the Book of Psalms as an eternal monument to the glory of God. He used the lyrics and the melodies of each song to persuade and convert others. David's music mission inspired his listeners to extol the God of Israel. Do you sing your praise songs as a musicianary or a celebrity? Is your purpose to seek fame or are you preparing praise songs to lead others to the faith?

David began his musicianary journey with Psalm 1. This song uses vivid, captivating poetry. David wrote, "Oh, the joys of those who do not follow the advice of the wicked, or stand around with sinners, or join in with mockers. But they delight in the law of the LORD, meditating on it day and night. They are like trees planted along the riverbank, bearing fruit each season. Their leaves never wither, and they prosper in all they do. But not the wicked! They are like worthless chaff, scattered by the wind" (Ps. 1:1–4, NLT). David draws a sharp contrast between the righteous and the wicked. The righteous do not hang out with and behave like the wicked. Instead they read and meditate on the Bible every day. Do you read your Bible daily and use it as a muse for your praise music? Or is your sanctuary worship clouded by the chaos of secular sensations? Jesus testified to the supremacy of Psalms even after His resurrection. Jesus appeared to His disciples and said, "These are the words which I spoke to you while I was still with you, that all things must be fulfilled which were written in the Law of Moses and the Prophets and the Psalms concerning Me" (Luke 24:44).

SANCTUARY PRAISE

It is no wonder that we are confused with regard to what type of music is suitable for the sanctuary. If we are not crystal clear on the advice of the righteous versus the wicked, then our spiritual judgment will also be clouded. The temple was constructed by Solomon from the plans given to David by the Spirit (1 Chron. 28:11–12).

Our understanding of God's Spirit must come from His Word which lies deep within our hearts. I remember going to a church in New York City to present a worship seminar. This church had a reputation of offering some of the best praise music in the region. The congregation could boast of members

> It is the Spirit who builds and fills the temple in a cloud of God's glory, not a cloud of confusion.

who were famous recording artists and celebrated worship leaders. They were also renowned for being exuberant and "Spirit-filled." As I stood during the singing, awaiting my time to speak, I was surrounded by ear-splitting sounds. I tried to engage in the atmosphere, but I felt as though my head would explode. The words of the song were powerful, yet the piercing instruments and irritating sounds deflated their importance.

I felt myself becoming more introspective as the blaring music began to dim in my mind. Then in what sounded like a small whisper, I could hear these words in my heart, "These people honor me with their lips, but their heart is far from Me" (see Isa. 29:13). My heart sank as I realized that this music was not God honoring. The praise music was primarily focused on the artistry of the worship team. Yet pure praise emerges from a heart of devotion to God. When I approached the podium, I had completely forgotten the opening remarks I had prepared. Instead of what I came to say, I repeated what the Holy Spirit inspired me to say. I said, "When you worship with your **A-R-T** instead of your **H-E-A-R-T**, God cannot be praised because **H-E** is not in it." You could hear a pin drop as the sanctuary fell silent. My afternoon seminar was filled to overflowing. One thing is clear; our praise songs in the sanctuary should not be void of our Savior.

Jesus frequented the temple in His day, yet made it clear that we are the temple. After cleansing the temple from unwanted peddlers, Jesus told the Jews that His body is the temple. "Jesus answered them, 'Destroy this temple, and in three days I will raise it up'" (John 2:19, ESV). Then the Apostle Paul sheds light on how to glorify God in our body and spirit by describing our bodies as a temple. In 1 Corinthians 6:19, Paul writes, "Or do you not know that your body is the temple of the Holy Spirit *who* is in you, whom you have from God, and you are not your own?" So I assert that the model of the sanctuary which was the template for the temple provides further insight into how to select our songs of praise. Let's look at the sanctuary model through the Psalms to supply us with a biblical blueprint for sanctuary praise.

As musicians, first we must hone our ability to hear. In the 2015 Adult Sabbath School Bible Study Guide entitled *Proverbs,* Jacques Doukhan, Professor of Hebrew and Old Testament Exegesis at Andrews University Theological Seminary, shares, "The act of 'hearing' marks the first step in education. In Hebrew thought the seat of wisdom or of intelligence is located not in the brain, but in the ears. This implies that even before we seek to conceptualize or solve a problem, we first need to hear it. This means we need to listen. When Solomon asks for wisdom, he specifically asks for 'a listening heart' (1 Kings 3:9, literal translation)."[1] We must ask God for a listening heart. It is only through the Holy Spirit's wisdom that we can discern and prepare the proper songs for the sanctuary.

In his book *The New Worship: Straight Talk on Music and the Church,* Barry Liesch gives us the meaning of the temple furniture as it relates to our modern-day praise.[2] I have slightly adapted these meanings.

1. **Altar**: At the *altar* in the Outer Court the offering is wholly consumed and goes up in smoke to heaven, illustrating the need for total *consecration*.

2. **Laver**: The *laver,* the washing basin for the priests, speaks of our need for *cleansing* before we come into the presence of a holy God. "Who may ascend the hill of the LORD? Or who may stand in his holy place? He who has clean hands and a pure heart" (Ps. 24:3–4).

3. **Table of shewbread**: We see the *table of shewbread* in the Holy Place which foreshadows the Lord's Supper and reminds us that we come as a member of one body. We are a *community* in Christ.

4. **The Seven-branched golden candle sticks**: It burns continually, replenished by a continuous supply of oil (Zech. 4). It symbolizes the *Holy Spirit* which illuminates the Word of God and enables us to perceive spiritual things (1 Cor. 2:12).

5. **The Altar of incense**: The altar stands in front of the veil now torn open, a symbol of *prayer* and the gateway to the Holy of Holies. It typifies the risen Christ offering prayers on our behalf before the throne. His prayers, along with ours commingled, rise as sweet perfume before the Lord.

6. **The Ark of the covenant**: The ark is in the Holy of Holies (Most Holy Place). The adoring cherubim guard the ark; the wooden chest overlaid with gold inside and out represents the presence of God. On the mercy seat, the lid of the chest, we see sprinkled blood, the price paid for our forgiveness by the completed work of Christ. Inside is where God's *covenant* law lies within our hearts.

God designed the temple furniture to symbolize Christ's ministry and reveal His presence in our lives. Each piece of furniture points our hearts and minds to the sacrifice of Jesus Christ. It is our faith in Jesus which justifies us to come into God's presence with clean hands and pure hearts (Ps. 24:4; Rom. 1:17). So today as we enter into the sanctuary, we can envision this ancient model. As a congregation, we humbly approach God in our hearts. In our acts of praise and worship, we acknowledge our need for *consecration, cleansing, community,* the *Holy Spirit, prayer,* and God's *covenant* that is shared in His Word. Our praise does not end when the worship service is over. Because we are the temple, our hearts and minds can be filled with perpetual praise as we abide in Christ and His Holy Word daily.

Furthermore, the ancient sanctuary gives us guidelines to select our music for worship: "Judson Cornwall, a Pentecostal worship writer from the late '70s and '80s promoted the idea that the worship leader can take the people on a worship journey that mirrors the 'Journey into the Holy of Holies' at every point. He cited Psalm 100 as scriptural support. The leader, he said, must know where the people are, where he wants to take them, and when they have arrived."[3] Cornwall's "worship progression" has five phases. I have modified these phases for the sanctuary service.

FIRST PHASE: SONGS OF PERSONAL TESTIMONY IN THE CAMP (JUBILATION)

Cornwall advises us to "meet the worshiper where they are, outside the gates in the camp."[4] These songs of gathering begin our worship service. As worshipers, first we focus on ourselves. We realize that despite our sins, we are redeemed. As a result, we sing for joy! We express our grateful hearts to God for His salvation through irrepressible gladness and humble service. We enter into God's presence with our minds on our personal problems yet become a witness as our songs testify to the power of God in our lives. These songs of jubilation can be hymns, choruses, CCM songs, inspirational, gospel, or spiritual tunes. The focus of these songs is personal and exuberant because here we testify of Jesus' love.

SECOND PHASE: THROUGH THE GATES WITH THANKSGIVING (THANKSGIVING)

Cornwall states, "The procession through the eastern gate into the outer court should be a joyful march, for thanks should never be expressed mournfully."[5] This is where our praise becomes practical as we thank God for the things He has done. It is a time of joy and boundless gratitude for God's goodness. Here is where our thoughts turn from personal problems to thankful praise. In this phase, our songs focus on what God has done for us. Our gratefulness becomes a grand musical gesture of profound devotion and praise.

THIRD PHASE: INTO HIS COURTS WITH PRAISE (PRAISE)

In this phase, Cornwall observes, "The emphasis changes from what God has done to who he is, to blessing his name and thinking less of one's self and more of God."[6] This is where our praise begins to swell and overflow. In this phase, we are aware of our frailties and celebrate God's infinite love, mercy, sovereignty, and grace. Here is where we sing our songs of praise in which the gospel of Jesus Christ and the power of God take precedence. In these songs, style is *still* not the primary emphasis. It is our praise to God for our salvation that grips our hearts.

FOURTH PHASE: SOLEMN WORSHIP INSIDE THE HOLY PLACE (AWE)

In the last two phases, our minds and hearts are focused only on the Trinity: God the Father, Jesus Christ, and the Holy Spirit. Here is where Cornwall becomes a pioneer as one of the first writers to make a clear distinction between "praise" and "worship." He explains, "'Praise' occurs in the outer court during the beginning of the service, whereas authentic, profound 'worship' takes place later in the inner court."[7] Here is where we encounter Jesus Christ interceding for our sins. Here we experience awe in that God's love for us results in the ministry of Jesus Christ to the world (John 3:16). This is where awe, sobriety, and reverence replace lightness. Here, in the presence of God, is where we enter into worship.

FIFTH PHASE: IN THE MOST HOLY PLACE (ADORATION)

In the last phase, we are in God's presence. Here we express our deepest love and devotion through adoration. Cornwall explains, "If the leader has been successful in bringing the people step by step into the outer court and on through it into the holy place, there will be a rise in the spiritual response of the people. Instead of mere soulish, emotional responses, there will be responses from the human spirit that have depth and devotion in them."[8] It is at this phase of worship that I feel the lyrics to Bart Millard's song "I Can Only Imagine" expresses our devotion to God and the diversity of our hearts.[9] He writes,

> Surrounded by Your glory
>   What will my heart feel
> Will I dance for You Jesus
>   Or in awe of You be still
> Will I stand in Your presence
>   Or to my knees will I fall
> Will I sing hallelujah
>   Will I be able to speak at all
> I can only imagine.

So in the sanctuary, our musical message should take us on a journey from *jubilation, thanksgiving, praise,* and *awe,* on to *adoration* of our Lord and Savior, Jesus Christ. Our response as we travel on the way to glory is pure praise and deep, sincere worship.

HEARTFELT PRAISE

While I continue to state that style and genre should not be the emphasis of our praise and worship music, we all know that in many regions around the world the topic of musical style is terrorizing the church. Wars waged over musical style may even be plaguing your church. How can we uncover what style of music is appropriate for sanctuary praise? The Bible tells us that God is a Creator (Gen. 1:1; John 1:3), and Satan is a corruptor (Ezek. 28:17). God created everything! Satan hasn't created anything! Satan did not create music. Satan can only corrupt music so it becomes a counterfeit. So if we know this, then why do we give Satan the creative credit so often? Satan's goal is to take the good things that God created and corrupt them. Music was Satan's gift when he was Lucifer in heaven (Ezek. 28:13–15). Since Satan sinned and was evicted from heaven, it is now his sole goal to corrupt music here on Earth. Satan has spiritual forces (Eph. 6:12, ESV) that can beguile us. So we must ensure that our music is filled with the power of the Holy Spirit and not the mayhem of counterfeit spiritual forces that will deceive us. Just because our praise music is spirited does not mean that it is spiritual.

> Our praise music must be *spiritual* and not just *spirited*.

Whatever we put deep into our hearts shapes our characters. The music that we listen to is reflected in the contents of our hearts and minds. I submit we should draw the same sharp contrasts today as David did in the past. As Christians, we must be clear on what music is acceptable to the hearts and minds of the righteous versus the ungodly. All successful songwriters have a technique that they use to craft music that is memorable, meaningful, and emotional. David was no exception. His Holy Spirit inspired techniques for writing the Book of Psalms has made his lyrics legendary for thousands of years. What an astounding legacy!

Music is powerful because it has the ability to influence our thoughts and shape our emotions which in turn affects our behavior. Patrik Juslin and John Sloboda, writers of *Music and Emotion: Theory and Research* share, "It is an ancient, and very pervasive idea that music *expresses* emotion. Apart from the copious literature to this effect contributed by composers, musicologists, and philosophers, there is also solid empirical evidence from psychological research, that listeners often agree rather strongly about what type of emotion is expressed in a particular piece. It is also a pervasive belief that music can, at times, actually produce emotion in listeners."[10] Therefore, music speaks to the heart, and the heart can speak from our music. Music enables us to become emotionally connected to situations and experiences we encounter. You will admit that if you experience something when a song was playing, like a wedding, first date, or graduation party, you will always remember your experience when you hear that song replayed. Music is memorable and powerful.

So we must utilize the gift of music with great care in our sacred settings. How can we ensure that our praise is heartfelt and Spirit-led? What kind of musical selections would produce appropriate praise? In Matthew 22, Jesus Himself gives us a clue to this quandary. Jesus Christ was called the "Son of David" (Matt. 1:1; 21:9; Mark 12:35). Yet, Jesus admits that David in the Spirit called Christ his Lord. "While the Pharisees were gathered together, Jesus asked them, saying, 'What do you think about the Christ? Whose Son is He?' They said to Him, 'The Son of David.' He said to them, 'How then does David in the Spirit call Him "Lord?"'" (Matt. 22:41–43). David was in the Spirit, so he knew Christ was Lord of all. Likewise, it is the Holy Spirit who revealed to David the components of appropriate praise that enabled him to pen the psalms. It is still the Holy Spirit who continues to reveal to us today what music is appropriate for praise.

God created music to possess characteristics that are similar to His own nature. The Holy Spirit is both universal (Joel 2:28) and personal (Gal. 4:6). In a similar fashion, music is both universal and personal. Music speaks to many people at the same time—in a universal manner. Music also addresses each individual in a very personal way according to his or her own experience, needs, and sensitivity—in a particular manner. In her book *In Tune with God*, Dr. Lilliane Doukhan writes, "What characterizes art, and music in particular, is that while it has the ability to speak to everybody in general, it speaks differently to each individual."[11] I'm sure you have experienced how music is both universal and yet personal. Most likely you have experienced this phenomenon for yourself. You can attend a worship service, and everyone in the congregation collectively hears a song that is written as a grand selection. Yet when you ask people's personal opinions, the music could be described as lifeless and terrible by one person and moving and beautiful by another.

In Psalm 22:3, David writes that God inhabits praise. Whatever God inhabits becomes like Him and takes on His divine nature. So we must ask, "What is God's divine nature?" When Jesus summarized the Ten Commandments (Exod. 20), He revealed God's nature. Jesus tells us that the law boils down to love for God and love for people (Matt. 22:37–39). God is Love (1 John 4:8). So love is a chief characteristic of God's nature.

The Apostle Paul gives us other aspects of God's nature by describing the fruit of the Spirit. In Galatians 5:22–23 (ESV), he writes, "But the fruit of the Spirit is love, joy, peace, patience, kindness, goodness, faithfulness, gentleness, self-control; against such there is no law." Therefore music that evokes the same *emotions* as the Spirit is suitable for the sanctuary. Instrumental music that makes us feel love and joy, brings about peaceful thoughts, produces a kind, gentle spirit, strengthens our faith, results in good behavior, produces patience, and motivates self-control is suitable for the sanctuary.

> Persuasive lyrics that invade the mind with the
> glory and majesty of God can be combined with
> pure melodies that stimulate Spirit-filled emotions
> such as love, joy, peace, patience, kindness, good-
> ness, faithfulness, gentleness, and self-control.

These sacred songs of praise are not burdened by style. They comprise only one genre. This genre combines lyrics and melodies that give all glory and honor to the majesty of God by extolling His divine nature, and then uses a culturally relevant, God-inspired instrumental music to attract those that He wishes to save.

Let's say that you are in a worship service and the music has beautiful melodies which make you feel good, peaceful, and loved. If the lyrics are vague and don't give clear indications that the song is addressing God (with words like God, Jesus, Holy Spirit, Lamb, sacrifice, grace, redeemed, restored, etc.), then that song can be easily mistaken for a secular love song. The reverse is also true; if you are listening to grand lyrics that glorify God yet the instrumental music elicits emotions that cause frustration, discord, impatience, anger, bitterness, sadness, lust, sensuality, and lack of self-control, etc., then the music may create a response in your heart that is lacking Christ's redemptive power. Now, we don't have to wage war and worry about what style of music to use in church! If the music has lyrics that extol God's majesty and melodies filled with Holy Spirit emotions, then it is suitable and will transform us into His image. This sacred music will not contain lyrics, beats, chords, or melodies that produce negative behaviors like anger, frustration, lust, sensuality, self-centeredness, impatience, or lack of self-control. These emotions and actions would not be in line with the Holy Spirit. They will create mental mayhem. Light cannot commune with darkness (2 Cor. 6:14).

It is the Holy Spirit who allows us to discern the melodies that offer pure praise. Maybe right now you are thinking that this rationale sounds too simplistic, idealistic, or far-fetched. How can we know the sounds of love, peace, or joy? We all watch movies, don't we? Try this at home. Focus on listening to the music when you are watching a movie. You can tell when the characters are really in love by the sound of the music even before you see the scene. You can tell whether the scene will be funny, suspenseful, or sad by the music that is played. You can also tell when the scene will be scary by the sound of the music. Isn't that true? Well, if we can do all of that by listening to the sound of secular music, why are we so baffled by the sound of sacred music? Is it the sound that is confusing or our determination to cling to traditions, rituals, and preferences that cloud our judgment?

It seems that the entertainment industry is not the only enterprise that recognizes the power of music. Even the automobile industry uses acoustical design to its advantage. The automakers of "BMW: The Ultimate Driving Machine" have hired a group of sound design engineers who make sure that what the drivers hear is suited to the car they are driving. When you open the door to the 7 Series BMW, their acoustical engineers assure us that the sound you hear announces a luxurious ride. Likewise, for the 5 or 6 Series BMW the sound that you hear while driving communicates a sporty ride. When it comes to the sound design at BMW, Dr. Alfred Zeitler, BMW's acoustic psychologist, tells us, "Even small changes to vehicle sound can have a big impact, since human hearing subconsciously evaluates acoustic surroundings like a high-performance analyser, and all changes are continuously registered in the brain."[12] Likewise, God has given us the Holy Spirit as a high-performance "analyzer" of the music we play in church. We must have an ear and learn to hear what the Spirit says to our churches (Rev. 2:28). (For more research, see Appendix II: The Meaning of Music.)

In his devotional book titled *Taste and See,* John Piper sums up our purpose for worship. He writes, "Worship is the term we use to cover all the acts of the heart and mind and body that intentionally express the infinite worth of God. This is what we were created for, as God says in Isaiah 43:7, 'Everyone who is called by My name, and whom I *have created for My glory…*' That means that we are all created to express the infinite worth of God's glory. We were created to worship."[13] Worship in Solomon's temple was a reflection of the glory and majesty of the presence of God. It took seven years to build and was done with the utmost attention to detail. Solomon assembled the elders of Israel, the heads of the tribes, and the chief fathers of the children of Israel. They all came to Jerusalem as the ark of the covenant was brought from Zion, the City of David (2 Chron. 5:2).

The animal sacrifices offered by the multitude were too great to number. Then the priest brought the ark to its place in the inner sanctuary of the temple, the Most Holy Place, the heart of the grand design. Nothing was placed in the ark except the two tablets of the covenant which Moses put there at Horeb when the children of Israel left Egypt. Then the people were unified as one body. When the focus of the congregation, priests, Levites, and music was centered solely on glorifying God, the results were majestic. This is what a sanctuary service filled with Holy Spirit power and pure praise looked like in ancient times:

> And it came to pass when the priest came out of the Most Holy Place (for all the priests who were present had sanctified themselves, without keeping to their divisions), and the Levites who were the singers, all those of Asaph and Heman and Jeduthun, with their sons and their brethren, stood at the east end of the altar, clothed in white linen, having cymbals, stringed instruments and harps, and with them one hundred and twenty priests sounding with trumpets—indeed it came to pass, when the trumpeters and singers were as one, to make one sound to be heard in praising and thanking the LORD, and when they lifted up their voice with the trumpets and cymbals and instruments of music, and praised the LORD, saying: "For He is good, For His mercy endures forever," that the house, the house of the LORD, was filled with a cloud, so

that the priests could not continue ministering because of the
cloud; for the glory of the LORD filled the house of God.
—2 CHRONICLES 5:11–14

Jeremiah 3:15 (KJV) says, "And I will give you pastors according
to mine heart, which shall feed you with knowledge and understanding." I pray that these revelations of musical majesty will
pierce, strengthen, and guide your heart.

LEVITE LESSONS

1. Private time in praise to God is paramount. But more
   importantly, submission to God's authority is the key
   to ministry success.

2. Our sole purpose as music ministers is to lift up Jesus
   Christ. We do this by creating a sermon in song that
   will draw people into God's presence.

3. Our understanding of God's Spirit must come from
   His Word which lies deep within our hearts.

4. Whatever we put deep into our hearts shapes our
   characters.

5. Music that evokes the same *emotions* as the Spirit is
   suitable for the sanctuary.

6. If the music has lyrics that extol God's majesty and
   melodies filled with Holy Spirit emotions, then it is
   suitable and will transform us into His image.

PRACTICAL PRAISE QUESTION

Is the praise music that you select for the sanctuary filled with Holy
Spirit power or counterfeit spiritual forces?

ENDNOTES

1. Jacques B. Doukhan, *Proverbs* (Nampa, ID: Pacific Press, 2014), 15.
2. Barry Liesch, *The New Worship: Straight Talk on Music and the Church* (Grand Rapids, MI: Baker Books, 2001), 68–69.
3. Ibid., 71.
4. Ibid.
5. Ibid.
6. Ibid., 72.
7. Ibid.
8. Ibid., 73.
9. Bart Millard, "I Can Only Imagine," Simpleville Music, 2001, 2002.
10. Patrik N. Juslin and John A. Sloboda, eds., *Music and Emotion: Theory and Research* (New York, Oxford: Oxford UP, 2001) 361.
11. Lilliane Doukhan, *In Tune with God* (Hagerstown, MD: Autumn House Pub., 2009), 57.
12. Sam Abuelsamid, "BMW Pursuing Better Acoustics to Improve Efficiency," May 2010, http://www.autoblog.com/2010/05/20/bmw-pursuing -better-acoustics-to-improve-efficiency/, accessed on February 8, 2015.
13. John Piper, *Taste and See: Savoring the Supremacy of God* (Sisters, OR: Multnomah, 2005), 58.

Chapter 6

I SURRENDER ALL

Whoever desires to come after Me, let him deny himself, and take up his cross and follow Me.

—MARK 8:34

PERSONAL PRAISE

*I*T SEEMED LIKE just another day in the desert. John waited patiently for the people to arrive as the arid air and sand pellets scraped his brow. He knew they were coming. Each day that he made his home in the Judean desert, more of the multitude came to hear his words and to be baptized. John had been preaching in the wilderness for months now. When he left home, his father Zacharias and mother Elizabeth knew they could not dissuade him. It was his destiny to prepare the way of the Lord (Luke 1:76). So he surrendered himself and all life's modern comforts for this purpose. He became a wanderer wearing only clothes woven from coarse camel hair with a leather belt around his waist. His food of locusts and wild honey was primitive and barely palatable. Yet he remained a preacher in the parched, burning sand preparing for the Messiah who would bring living water.

Then the people came—Pharisees, Sadducees, publicans, tax collectors, soldiers, and the town's people from Judea and Jerusalem; each one came to hear John preach in the wilderness. He gave each person individual instructions when asked, "What shall we do then?" (Luke 3:10–14). John's preaching heralded one constant refrain, "Repent, for the kingdom of heaven is at hand!" (Matt. 3:1–2). Sincere repentance was needed for the Israelites to experience the revelation of God and truly reverence his Messenger—the Christ. As the people came, the crowd grew. John held a grand evangelistic meeting that fine day. All the people who came to the desert thirsting for truth were baptized in the water of the Jordan River. Yet John knew there was much more to his ministry. "And he preached saying, 'There comes One after me who is mightier than I, whose sandal strap I am not worthy to stoop down and loose. I indeed baptized you with water, but He will baptize you with the Holy Spirit'" (Mark 1:7–8).

The next day as John began to prepare the people for baptism, he saw a familiar face coming in the distance. It was his cousin, Jesus of Nazareth. John could see the glow of God's glory on Jesus' face. So he exclaimed to the crowd, "Look! The Lamb of God who takes away the sin of the world! He is the one I was talking about when I said, 'A man is coming after me who is far greater than I am, for he existed long before me.' I did not recognize him as the Messiah, but I have been baptizing with water so that he might be revealed to Israel" (John 1:29–31, NLT). Jesus came from Galilee to be baptized. John protested, knowing that Jesus should baptize him and not vice versa. Yet Jesus assured him that this was necessary to fulfill all righteousness (Matt. 3:15).

So Jesus went down deep that day. He surrendered His body into the muddy waters of the Jordan River so He could be baptized. Jesus lived a lifestyle of worship. Even in His opening acts of ministry, Jesus demonstrated that the temple of God was in Him. In His act of personal praise, He *consecrated* His heart so that His symbolic *cleansing* could be seen by the entire *community*. After coming out of the water, Jesus knelt on the riverbank to *pray*: "And immediately, coming up from the water, He saw the heavens parting and the *Spirit* descending upon Him like a dove. Then a voice came from heaven, 'You are My beloved Son, in whom I am well pleased'" (Mark 1:10–11). God the Father interceded to signify that Jesus had begun His ministry fulfilling His *covenant* promise with His Son (Isa. 42:1).

The call of God is magnificent! It must have been marvelous for Jesus to have God's visible and audible seal of approval given to Him in full public view. How miraculous it must have been to see a dove fly from the heavens in the middle of the desert to land on Jesus. Clearly the crowd had to notice something was different about Jesus' baptism. Yet it's not clear if everyone saw the dove or heard the voice of God at the shores of the Jordan River that day. But John bore witness to the event saying, "I saw the Spirit descending from heaven like a dove, and He remained upon Him. I did not know Him, but He who sent me to baptize with water said to me, 'Upon whom you see the Spirit descending, and remaining on Him, this is He who baptizes with the Holy Spirit.' And I have seen and testified that this is the Son of God" (John 1:32–34).

I am sure there are times you can remember when God ordained your ministry through miraculous means. We all have a story. While I was attending college in the mid-1980s, I began singing with a six-member, female gospel group named Reconciled. At first, singing with Reconciled was something fun to do with my girl-friends. We all loved to sing Christian music, and we all had been singing either as soloists, in small groups, or in choirs all of our lives. After a few years together, we had completed our undergrad-uate degrees and now had successful corporate careers. We believed singing Christian music was the most wonderful hobby imaginable! But it turned out that the Holy Spirit had other plans. He was with us, and each engagement brought us more and more popularity. At first, we sang in small local churches. Next, we sang in larger churches throughout our region. Then, we began to travel to other nearby states. Eventually, our schedules became full with church engagements and concerts along the east coast. Finally, rehearsals and engagements for Reconciled started to monopolize our time. But we absolutely loved it!

We began to secure larger-than-life engagements at places like Lincoln Center in New York City, the Kennedy Center in Washington, D.C., and Bobby Jones Gospel Show in Nashville,

Tennessee. We were the opening act for mainstream gospel artists like CeCe Winans, The Richard Smallwood Singers, Take 6, Daryl Coley, The Hawkins Family, Twinkie Clark, and many more. We won first prize in the Gospel Amateur Night at the world-famous Apollo Theatre in Harlem, New York. People began to recognize us in stores, shopping malls, and around town. It was a dream come true. We asked ourselves what could be better than a music ministry that is fun, lets us hang with people we love, and sing music that we all enjoy? At first, popularity and fame are always pleasant. Who doesn't love to be praised and celebrated? But what about the hardships that come with the call to ministry? What happens when you have to surrender all in your wilderness?

"Then Jesus, full of the Holy Spirit, returned from the Jordan River. He was led by the Spirit in the wilderness, where he was tempted by the devil for forty days. Jesus ate nothing all the time and became very hungry" (Luke 4:1–2, NLT). It is often right after we experience the most glorious highs in our personal ministry that the devil comes to tempt and deceive us. We are led into the wilderness where trials devour our faith and leave us hungering for help and righteous relief. Most times we attribute these trials to the craftiness of the devil and his evil ways. But the Bible makes it clear that *it was the Spirit who led Jesus into the wilderness.* How many times have you been blessed by life's experiences, just to find yourself in the next moment thrown down into utter despair? You find yourself led by the Spirit into your wilderness.

> Often when we are blessed, God uses spiritual stress as a means to test our faith (1 Kings 19).

Jesus was tempted by the devil in three ways. Jesus was tempted regarding His passion for life (turn stones into bread); His power to save (throw yourself down); and His worship allegiance (fall down and worship me) (see Matt. 4:1–8). These temptations were waged by the devil to distract Jesus from His ministry and place Him outside of God's will. However, Jesus won His epic battle against Satan with the weapon of God's Word. He surrendered His thoughts and will and only responded to Satan with Scripture. *The Nelson Study Bible* commentary explains,

> Jesus' response to all three temptations was to quote the Word of God showing His followers the power of Scripture in battling the Evil One (see Deut. 6:13; 8:3; Ps. 91:11–12). There was nothing *morally* wrong with turning stones into bread; Satan was tempting Jesus to do a miracle outside of the Father's will. This explains why Jesus quotes Deuteronomy 8:3. Bread alone does not sustain life; ultimately, God is the One who sustains all life. Thus it is our responsibility to trust God and remain in His will. In quoting the protective promise of Psalm 91:11–12 to Jesus, Satan omitted the words "to keep you in all your ways." Satan tempted Jesus to gain public attention through spectacle rather than through His righteous life and message. Christ rebuked the devil for asking for worship, a temptation to do the opposite of what every Israelite was called upon to do (Deut. 6:13, 15). Specifically in reference to Jesus, Satan was offering a crown without the Cross.[1]

So often in our music ministries we may be tempted to go outside of God's will. We are tempted with our passion for a successful life in the music industry. Because of this passion, we will do anything in our power to save and maintain our music careers. If this persists, eventually we end up trading our worship allegiance. We worship the music, or worse, ourselves—instead of our Savior. The thrill of fame can be alluring. When tempted, we chase after the fame and approval of the crowd instead of faith in the Cross of Christ. When we are in God's will, even our fame will have spiritual influence. God uses fame as a means to showcase and strengthen our faith. God uses our fame as a way to promote His glory. We cannot have a crown without a cross. We cannot have glory without the grind. Our lives must endure sacrifice and suffering for God to truly test us and use us for His glory (see 2 Tim. 3:12). When times of temptations and trials come, do you surrender your will and respond with God's Word, or do you just follow your own way?

After several years of successful singing with Reconciled, we had the opportunity to consider a record deal. We had always been united in our music and our friendships, yet when this opportunity for fame arose, we could no longer agree. We had months of intense discussions on which path to take. Finally we decided to maintain our friendships and careers and ignore the record deal offers. As time passed, member commitment waned and major engagements began to lessen. Our relationships became strained, and finally members just quit singing. The call of God that was on our lives for music ministry was never fully realized through Reconciled. Back then, it made sense to me to pursue a record deal on our own terms or just continue singing as we had been. We were happy for over seven years. But sadly it never occurred to me that my decision was self-centered and not ministry-minded. I didn't ask God what did He desired for my life. I never thought to weigh this offer for fame against God's Word in faith. The aftermath of my decision—to leave the group and live outside of God's will—was costly. My charmed life entered a tail spin of disappointment, unexpected hardships, financial ruin, and a ministry vacuum. All because when I was tempted, I decided to follow my own way instead of answering Christ's call to "Follow Me."

Worship is a lifestyle of surrendered obedience, not just a sweet serenade.

Have you ever been in a similar situation? Have you missed Christ's humble call to "Follow Me," and instead followed after the music or the worship whims of the masses? How can we surrender all and humbly follow Christ? The simple answer is we must devote ourselves to worshiping Him *alone*. More than anything else in life, we must long to be in God's presence. Like John's call in the wilderness, before we can follow Christ, we must first repent of our sins. Many of us have become self-centered in our worship practice. Our worship is limited to artistry while our lives lack ministry.

We cannot continue to act as if worship is limited to the few minutes of music that precede our church services. I am even convinced we cannot continue to classify worship as simply the church service! True worship resounds in a lifestyle of seeking and serving the Savior.

Let's see how several scriptures in Psalms describe the worshiper's closeness to God.

Worship Texts in Psalm	Worshiper's Closeness to God
1. Psalm 22:27, 29	Worship and bow before You
2. Psalm 86:9	Worship before You
3. Psalm 95:6	Worship, bow down and kneel before the LORD
4. Psalm 96:9	Tremble before Him
5. Psalm 99:5, 9	Worship at His footstool
6. Psalm 138:2	Worship toward Your holy temple

None of the texts equate worship with music! You can continue this exercise for yourself, and you will see that the Hebrew word for *worship* in the Book of Psalms is not musical in nature. Instead, all of these texts illustrate that the worshiper is in the presence of God. The worshiper desires to reverence his Creator by drawing near. Somehow in our understanding of worship today, we have lost our desperate desire to be in God's presence. We are more concerned with a concept of worship based on musical style and our personal preference. Consequently, we all must repent of our erroneous, self-serving ways and surrender our lives anew to Jesus Christ (Matt. 4:17).

But be aware, this total surrender is no easy path. This path is not paved with roses. When you surrender all to follow Christ, you have chosen a path of hardship and strife that opposes culture. When everyone around you equates music to worship, your contrary position will not be popular. It is a difficult, lonely journey—especially when at times it seems like all roads in Christian music lead to the American idol of worship stardom and sacrificial fame. You see, it was no accident that Satan used the lyrics of a song to tempt Jesus (Ps. 91:11–12). It was not accidental that Satan's final temptation was "fall down and worship me" (Matt. 4:9). That is still his final temptation to us today. Many times his temptations are shrouded in the lyrics or melodies of our songs. Satan's ultimate temptation is for us to fall down and worship him. When we are self-absorbed and out of God's will, even our "worship" can take us on a downward spiral.

The Greek word Satan used for worship was *proskynēo*. It means "to kiss the hand (toward) one, in token of reverence."[2] Primarily, this worship was an act of profound reverence among the Persians who fell down on the ground or prostrated themselves to show their allegiance to a ruler. Satan desires that same kind of worship allegiance from us. First he wants us to fall down. We do this when we lower our standards and lower our guard against sin. The Word of God is no longer the weapon we use to fight the devil's deceptions. We have substituted our own ways and will for God's Word. We rely on our personal preference for protection. We use musical style as our standard. Then, void of God's Word, it is easy to worship anything and everything. Unfortunately, when we neglect God's Word, we choose to follow Satan's plan. We fall down into the deep abyss of self-reliance where our worship amounts to idolatry and utter chaos.

However, in Jesus there is always help and hope! In Jesus, the devil's deceptions are defeated. This same word for worship, *proskynēo*, is the word that Jesus used to describe true worship and service to God (Matt. 4:10). This kind of worship also describes an intimacy (kissing the hand) that can only be achieved when you are very close to someone. We must become intimate with Jesus through studying Scripture and meditating on His Word. This is the only way we can truly know our Savior. Our songs must not be used to soothe our suffering or as a substitute for intimate worship. In true worship, our praise songs become the sound of victory, for we know the war against sin has been won! World-renowned vocalist and education activist Pastor Wintley Phipps shares his understanding of the profound purpose of suffering: "It is in the quiet crucible of our personal, private suffering that our noblest dreams are born and God's greatest gifts are given and often. God gives His greatest gifts in compensation for what we've been through."[3]

Jesus also used this same word *proskyneo* when he spoke to the woman at the well (John 4:20–24). This intimacy and abandonment that requires total surrender to God is our truest worship. It is words of life, not just lyrics to songs that give us power to overcome Satan's seductions. The old gospel hymn says, "Nothing between my soul and the Savior"; not even our songs should get in our way. Hold on to God! Remember, often it is the Spirit who leads you into your desert where wilderness woes can consume your life. When you are in your wilderness, be like Jesus and use the Word of God as your weapon. Then you will always be victorious! The lesson that Jesus taught us in the wilderness is to surrender all to God. Rev. 22:17 says, "And the Spirit and the bride say, 'Come!' And let him who hears say, 'Come!' And let him who thirsts come. Whoever desires, let him take the water of life freely." I pray that your worship will be watered by the power of God's Word. Let our truest worship be a surrendered life that is always thirsting and seeking after God.

PRAISE POWER

After the wilderness, the Holy Spirit led Jesus back to Galilee to begin His ministry. The news about Jesus' supernatural baptism spread far and wide, and crowds of people began to follow Him. So when Jesus entered His hometown of Nazareth, as usual, He went to the synagogue on the Sabbath. Each Sabbath the synagogue reading taken from the Law and the Prophets was predetermined.

Jesus stood up to read the scroll. The reading from the Prophet Isaiah was prepared and handed to Him by the attendant.

> And He opened the book and found the place where it was written, "The Spirit of the Lord is upon Me, because He had anointed Me to preach the gospel to the poor. He has sent Me to proclaim release to the captives, and recovery of sight to the blind, to set free those who are oppressed, to proclaim the favorable year of the Lord." And He closed the book, gave it back to the attendant and sat down; and the eyes of all in the synagogue were fixed on Him. And He began to say to them, "Today this Scripture has been fulfilled in your hearing."
> —LUKE 4:16–21, NASB

Jesus' life was a testimony of powerful praise to God. Jesus was filled with the Holy Spirit. As a result, He offered Himself as a living sacrifice holy and acceptable to both God and men (Rom. 12:1). It was the anointing of the Holy Spirit that empowered Him and enlivened His messianic ministry. Therefore, Jesus' ministry was evidence by His actions. Scripture declares it was because Jesus was anointed by the Spirit that He came to preach the gospel to the poor, release the captives, restore sight to the blind, free the oppressed, and proclaim the Lord's favor. Jesus' praise was palpable.

Psalm 40:3 explains, "He has put a new song in my mouth— praise to our God; many will *see it* and fear, and trust in the LORD." Notice that David says clearly that *people will* see, *not* hear, *your songs of praise.* The Israelites could see Jesus' praise. It was manifested in His life of service to others. Can people see your praise? Is your praise evident to the people around you who need the Lord? Is your life of praise filled with the Holy Spirit power to transform hearts and minds? Our praise power is not just singing each Sabbath on the platform where we can be seen. Our praise power is to use our position of leadership influence to see the needs of the people God has sent us to serve. On a WGTS 91.9 FM radio interview, Mike Donehey, lead singer of the group Tenth Avenue North, explained how to manage fame when ministering to the masses. He shared, "Jesus was always in a crowd. He spent much of His ministry surrounded by adoring fans. Yet when Jesus entered the crowd, He did not go to be *seen*. Jesus went into the crowd to *see*. He went into the crowd to see the needs of others and serve the people."[4]

Jesus went into the crowd with Holy Spirit power to identify the needs of the people. He came to seek and save the lost. Jesus went into the crowd to lead people into true worship—an intimate relationship with God the Father.

Today, our definition of the worship leader has become extremely narrow. We believe that worship leading means we are Holy Spirit anointed singers

Hence, Jesus is our Supreme Worship Leader (Heb. 7:24–25).

that lead the worship service with songs. However, musician and educator Dean Kurtz, author of the book *God's Word, The Final Word on Worship and Music,* broadly defines the worship leader as "All those who stand before God's people and with their words or songs direct our thoughts toward God."[5] This definition, if employed, would dramatically change our worship perspective. Imagine the power in our churches if everyone who sang, prayed, read Scripture, made announcements, taught the children's lesson, preached, and played an instrument considered themselves a worship leader because each one has a word or song that directs our thoughts to God.

Jesus is the One who leads us into the presence of God (John 14:6). However, it is what the Holy Spirit appointed Jesus to do that differs vastly from our view of worship leading and Holy Spirit anointing today. The list of activities that was demonstrated in Jesus' life due to His Holy Spirit anointing is key to a deeper understanding of praise power. Let's look closely at Jesus' ministry activities again. The Spirit of the Lord anointed Jesus to:

- Preach the gospel to the poor.
- Heal the brokenhearted.

- Proclaim liberty to the captives.

- Recover sight to the blind.

- Liberate the oppressed.

- Proclaim the acceptable year of the Lord.

Music is a central part of praise to God. Yet when we accept the position of worship leader, our influence should extend far beyond the music we sing. An anointed worship leader uses his or her life to minister. If your gift is music, then your songs are the means that enable you to preach the gospel to the poor in spirit, heal the broken hearted, free the captives from sin, give sight to those who can't see the Savior, liberate those oppressed by life's difficulties, and proclaim God's grace every year that you serve. Your life represents the life of Christ. Your songs become sermons. However, as worship leaders, many of us don't aspire to lead like Jesus. We seem to have settled for our songs just being good praise music while our lives lack the praise power to convict and convert.

Many times I have heard people wonder why we don't have the supernatural power like Jesus and His disciples. Yet Jesus assured us that we will do even greater things than He did (John 14:12). Maybe the problem is not that we don't *have* the power; maybe the problem is that we are not *connected* to the power. It is God's Word that reveals the condition of the hearts to heal, convert, and convict (Heb. 4:12). Without God's Word, we are empty. Without God's Word, our lives will not fully reflect the life of Jesus Christ. Without God's Word, our ministries may be popular but not powerful. In her book *Steps to Christ,* Ellen White writes, "Christ connects fallen man in his weakness and helplessness with the Source of Infinite power."[6] Worship leading is a high calling. It requires a heart and mind that is convicted and converted by the Holy Spirit to lead people into the matchless presence of God. Is that your goal when you stand up to sing each Sabbath? Do you desire to lead people into God's presence so they can hear the gospel and be healed? Is your life a living testimony? When people hear your praise songs, do they see and hear the Good News or just good sounds?

Jesus' convictions went against His congregation. They marveled at His authority to claim that the Scripture He read had just been fulfilled. Many of them said, "Isn't this Joseph's son?" (see Luke 4:22). They wondered if He would perform the miracles in their town that they heard He did in other regions. Yet in the end, they couldn't accept a hometown son as a priestly hero. As Jesus continued to expose their unbelief and lack of acceptance, the congregation turned into an angry mob. They led Him to the edge of town to kill Him by throwing Him off a cliff. Jesus' worship leading didn't make people feel good; on the contrary, it made them uncomfortable and angry. Christ's doctrines led them to take a hard look at their lives and reevaluate their beliefs. It cut to the core. In true worship, we are broken because the closer we get to God, the more we see our sinful condition (Isa. 6:1–5). Our praise is not just filled with feel-good music. It is overflowing with music that helps us to feel the goodness of God. As we strive to model our worship leadership after Jesus, the question remains, "Where does your praise music lead?"

It's not surprising that soon after Jesus' experience in the synagogue He called His disciples. The word *disciple,* though primarily a New Testament word, was also used in the Old Testament. First Chronicles 25:7–8 reads, "So the number of them, with their brethren who were instructed in the songs of the LORD, all who were skillful, was two hundred and eighty-eight. And they cast lots for their duty, the small as well as the great, the teacher with the student." The word *student* (*talmiyd* in the Greek) means a disciple, one taught.[7] This word *disciple* is used only twice in the Old Testament (1 Chron. 25:8; Isa. 8:16). In First Chronicles, the word *disciple* is used to describe the Levites who were the skilled sanctuary musicians. Therefore, it is clear that the Levites who were the sanctuary musicians were also called disciples. Even in ancient times before the ministry of Jesus Christ, discipleship was an integral part of the sanctuary service.

So Jesus went to the Sea of Galilee, and the crowds followed Him there. While He was on the shore preaching, He saw two empty boats. The fishermen who owned the boats had left to wash their nets. They had been fishing all night, but their efforts were futile. There were no fish to be found. Jesus got into Simon Peter's empty boat and asked if he would push off from the shore a bit so He could escape the crowd. Then Jesus continued to preach to the people from the boat. After His teaching, Jesus said to Simon, "Now go out where it is deeper and let down your nets to catch some fish" (Luke 5:4, NLT). Although Peter had probably been one of John's disciples (John 1:40) who believed that the Christ would soon appear, Jesus knew that it was time for Peter to go deeper. Jesus called Peter to go outside of his comfort zone. He commanded him to leave the water's shallow edge. How many times do we find ourselves comfortable in shallow worship waters? We are called into a deep relationship with God, but we resist giving up our spiritual comforts. So we remain close to the shore instead of diving deep into worship.

Peter explained to Jesus that there was no hope. He had been out all night, and they didn't catch any fish. Their attempts to capture fish had failed so miserably that they decided to divert their attention to washing the nets. Because they were in shallow water, no fish were to be found. Sometimes, like Peter, we feel hopeless with our offering of praise. We have done everything in our power to attract and captivate the people, but our efforts seem in vain. Because we are on shallow scriptural ground the people are not captivated by our message. Ultimately, we divert our attention away from the mission to the music. Like Peter, we remain on the shore fixing our nets when instead we should be mending our ways.

No matter what you think about Peter, one thing is true: he was a man of action. Although Peter doubted his own ability, he showed that he had faith in Jesus. His response demonstrated his surrender. He said, "'Master, we have toiled all night and caught nothing; nevertheless at Your word I will let down the net.' And when they had done this, they caught a great number of fish, and their net was breaking" (Luke 5:5–6). Peter may have lacked confidence in his own success, but he knew that Jesus' word could change his circumstances. His response "At Your word," was a statement of faith that Jesus' word had power. The result of his act of faith—to obey Jesus' word—was a boat full of fish. Peter surrendered his plans to Jesus, and the results were astonishing. After an entire night of fishing without catching one fish, now they had more than two boatloads of fish! The boats were so full that they began to sink. Peter realized that he was in the presence of God, so he fell down at Jesus' knees and exclaimed, "Depart from me, for I am a sinful man, O Lord! (Luke 5:8).

When Peter surrendered his will and experienced Jesus Christ as his Lord, he immediately felt the need to confess his sins. He was frightened and confused by the enormous catch that caused his boat to sink. Jesus calmly allowed Peter's boat to begin sinking before He would save him. Peter had to experience sinking before Jesus would save and select him for discipleship. Peter had to be humbled before Jesus would enable him to be exalted (1 Pet. 5:6). Many times before Jesus can use us for His glory, He will allow us to feel His power. This enables us to see ourselves as we truly are—mere humanity in the presence of divinity. After He revealed His divinity, Jesus lovingly assured Peter and responded to his fear by commissioning him as a disciple. "And Jesus said to Simon, 'Do not be afraid. From now on you will catch men.' So when they had brought their boats to land, they forsook all and followed Him" (Luke 5:10–11). It is not easy to change course and follow Jesus Christ. But when you do, the outcome will be life changing. When we, as worship leaders, are empowered by the Bible to follow Jesus Christ and surrender all, our words and songs will catch men for God's kingdom.

LEVITE LESSONS

1. Often when we are blessed, God uses spiritual stress as a means to test our faith (1 Kings 19).

2. When we are in God's will, even our fame will have spiritual influence.

3. True worship resounds in a lifestyle of seeking and serving the Savior.

4. We must become intimate with Jesus through studying Scripture and meditating on His Word. This is the only way we can truly know our Savior.

5. Our praise power is to use our position of leadership influence to see the needs of the people God has sent us to serve.

6. Jesus is our Supreme Worship Leader (Heb. 7:24–25).

7. When we, as worship leaders, are empowered by the Bible to follow Jesus Christ and surrender all, our words and songs will catch men for God's kingdom.

PRACTICAL PRAISE QUESTION

What are some practical ways that can you surrender your music ministry to Jesus Christ so that your worship will attract more followers to the kingdom of God?

ENDNOTES

1.   Earl D. Radmacher, Th. D., *The Nelson Study Bible* (Nashville: Thomas Nelson, 1997), 1581.

2.   *Blue Letter Bible,* s.v. *"proskynēo,"* http://www.blueletterbible.org/lang/lexicon/lexicon.cfm?Strongs=G4352&t=KJV, accessed on March 6, 2015.

3.   Pastor Wintley Phipps, phone discussion with author, Upper Marlboro, MD, March 13, 2015.

4.   Mike Donehey, Interview, WGTS 91.9 FM, "Morning Show with Jerry & Blanca," 23 February 2015.

5.   Dean Kurtz, *God's Word: The Final Word on Worship and Music* (Maitland, FL: Xulon Press, 2008), 6.

6.   Ellen G. White, *Steps to Christ* (Mountain View, CA: Pacific Press, 1948), 20.

7.   *Blue Letter Bible,* s.v. "talmiyd," http://www.blueletterbible.org /lang/lexicon/lexicon.cfm?Strongs=H8527&t=NKJV accessed on April 14, 2015.

Chapter 7

IN CHRIST ALONE

And I, if I be lifted up from the earth, will draw all men unto me.
—**JOHN 12:32**, KJV

MISSIONAL PRAISE

WITH SUCH LITTLE time and so much to do, Jesus maximized every moment of His three-year ministry. Although He was divinity wrapped in humanity, Jesus trained thirty years for His three-year assignment. Jesus was committed both to His divine purpose and to being properly prepared to fulfill it. By now, He had spent years tutoring all twelve of His disciples. Christ mentored each one to carry on His kingdom call.

He spent His time preaching, teaching, healing the sick, raising the dead, exorcizing demons, and forgiving sins. Jesus was God's Word personified (John 1:1). Jesus became a friend of sinners so He could free them from their bondage (Luke 19:1–8). He did all this with a singular mission in mind. His per-

> Jesus' ministry was mission driven.

sonal mission statement was clear, focused, and precise. Jesus said, "For the Son of Man came to seek and to save the lost" (Luke 19:10, NIV). What is your mission? Do you have a personal mission statement like Jesus? What has God called you to do?

As I began to realize that my life was out of God's divine order, I cried out to Him in earnest repentance. During the five years that passed while I was not singing or participating in any church ministry, I begged God daily for a second chance. I promised God that I would willingly do whatever He asked of me. No questions and no fear! I pledged to be faithful no matter what it took. Then I began to prepare myself to sing again as I thought I would. I took voice lessons. I spoke to my friends and fellow musicians about start-up singing groups in the area. To remain active, I joined a mass choir and became a church chorister. I was convinced that God would allow me to have a second chance to serve Him in song. However, be careful what you pray for! I prayed for a chance to serve in music, and this is exactly what God provided.

In June 2000, on a beautiful, sunny Sabbath day, I was sitting in the back of the school we rented while our sanctuary was being renovated. At that time, I attended the Community Praise Center SDA Church (CPC) under the leadership of Pastor Henry M. Wright. Back then, I often sat in the rear of the auditorium because my son was an active two year old. After the service, Pastor Wright walked up to me very casually and said he needed to talk to me. I said, "Sure, I have some time," as I stood up to greet him. Then he said something that I will never, ever forget. He explained that our music director was no longer serving and that the volunteer position was vacant. He said, "The Lord told me to ask you to be the minister of music." He paused slightly for effect as all good preachers do; then he continued. "Now, I am not asking you to be the music leader or music director, like we had before. I am asking you to be the minister of music for this church." When I heard the words exit his mouth, it shocked me. I fell down into my seat and had to take a deep breath. The words swirled around in my head. I thought to myself, "*The Lord told you to ask me to be the minister of music?*" In that moment, I knew my life would be forever changed. God had chosen my mission.

The only way that Jesus could accomplish His mission was to sacrifice everything. To set the captives free as He prophesied, Jesus had to endure suffering. He knew He had come to die. He mentioned His fate frequently to His disciples. The only way He could truly save humankind was if He was condemned and sentenced to death by the cruelest penalty—Roman crucifixion. The end of His ministry was drawing near. In His divine thoughts, Jesus saw that the end of time was also near. He began to share with His disciples signs of the end times (Matt. 24–25). It was only a few days before the Passover feast, and Jesus knew His crucifixion was close. Then after He had finished all these sayings, He spoke to His disciples and said, "You know that after two days is the Passover, and the Son of Man will be delivered up to be crucified" (Matt. 26:2).

While the disciples did not fully understand Jesus' sayings about His death, the church leaders were plotting by trickery to kill Him (Matt. 26:3–4). As a part of their scheme, the chief priest, elders, and scribes decided that they would wait until after the feast so that the people would not riot. The church leaders were more concerned about the response of people than surrendering their traditions so they could truly praise God (John 12:43). Are we like the ancient church leaders today? Are we more concerned about the people's responses or the church's traditions rather than giving God true praise? Do we plan programs that kill true worship in an effort to calm a riot in our pews? Be aware that Satan still uses trickery and gimmicks to deceive us. We are mesmerized by the bright lights and sensational sounds of the music. Yet without mission, our music lacks depth, produces mayhem, and will weaken our connection to Jesus Christ.

Meanwhile, Jesus traveled to the town of Bethany and stayed at Simon the Leper's home. While He was there, Mary, His devoted follower, was determined to express her adoration and praise. She poured a very expensive jar of perfume on Jesus' head and washed His feet with her hair (Matt. 26:7; John 12:3). Judas of Iscariot, the ministry treasurer, was annoyed and resented Mary's wasteful act. He complained that the money for the perfume should have been given to the poor (John 12:4–5). Jesus explained that this anointing was for His burial, and Mary's kind, loving act would be forever memorialized in the Gospel story (Matt. 26:13). It seemed as if Judas' concern for the misuse of funds drove him to betray Jesus. But do not be fooled by Judas' actions. Rebellion against God is not typically a singular, impulsive act. Sin often results after a long time of brooding over misplaced priorities, self-centered dreams, and self-reliant hopes. As musicians, we must give our priorities, dreams, and hopes to God.

Immediately, Judas went to Caiaphas, the high priest, and made plans to betray Jesus for a slave's wage—thirty pieces of silver (Exod. 21:32). What a contrast between Mary and Judas' actions. Judas, Jesus' chosen and trusted disciple, devalued Christ's life to a mere slave's wage, while Mary, a scorned woman of the world, honored and valued Jesus' life as a gift that was precious and priceless. How often do we, as musicians, devalue Christ's life through our actions or in our ministries? Do we act as if the gift of God is priceless, or are we resentful because at times we feel as if we are only receiving a slave's wage for our musical gifts? It is the grace of Jesus Christ that has the power to save sinners, not our own musical gifts and talents. In the presence of Jesus, we must yearn to be mission minded. We must purpose in our hearts to be more like Mary, a surrendered follower of Jesus Christ who doesn't count the cost.

On the first day of the Feast of Unleavened Bread, Jesus prepared to celebrate the Passover with His disciples. In divine fashion, Jesus revealed the location of a man who would supply them with an upper room in which to prepare the Passover Supper. Jesus sent ahead two of His disciples to prepare the meal. By evening, Jesus and the twelve were eating and celebrating the Passover. During their meal, Jesus shared that His betrayer was among them. After an unsuccessful inquiry from the twelve to discover the culprit, Jesus began to serve the Passover Supper bread and wine. At the end of their meal, Satan entered Judas and he left the room to betray Jesus (John 13:26–30). Often, it is our closest friends who betray us in ministry. When God blesses your ministry, your friends may become envious, resentful, petty, or jealous of the gifts that God has given you. Your closest friends may deceive you or sell you out. Your best friend may undermine your ministry or try to steal your position. However, in Christ, they can never pickpocket your peace! While suffering from the death of his fiancé and in utter despair, poet and hymn writer Joseph Scriven sent these words to his mother:

> What a friend we have in Jesus,
>> All our sins and griefs to bear!
> What a privilege to carry,
>> Everything to God in prayer!
> Oh, what peace we often forfeit,
>> Oh, what needless pain we bear.
> All because we do not carry,
>> Everything to God in prayer![1]

Jesus will be with you even when your closest friends forsake you. I know. I can testify. I was deeply hurt and betrayed by a dear friend in ministry. But now, I live triumphantly. Jesus is my best friend who brought me through my own music ministry betrayal and personal trials. Don't worry! No matter how difficult a situation may become in your music ministry or life, Jesus will be your best friend. Jesus will never leave you!

"Now there was also a dispute among them, as to which of them should be considered the greatest" (Luke 22:24). It is amazing how selfish we can be at times, even as worshipers. In times of distress and grief, we often tend to become completely self-absorbed. Jesus was about to suffer capital punishment. He was about to be crucified and give His life to save humankind. He had just been betrayed. Yet in this crucial moment, His remaining disciples were focused solely on themselves. Unbelievably, they argued about who among them would be the greatest. Their discussion was self-centered and frivolous despite the somber circumstances. They still didn't understand the seriousness of sin and the high price of redemption. Are we guilty of the same misunderstandings and selfishness today? People all around us are dying in sin. Yet we sit in church and dispute over which worship leader, praise team, pastor, or church fellowship is the greatest instead of sharing the Greatest Story ever told. Now is the time to be serious about our worship. Our praise must have the ability to penetrate beyond the walls of the church in order to change the world. "And when they had sung a hymn, they went out to the Mount of Olives" (Matt. 26:30).

> Even in the face of death, Jesus led His disciples in musical praise.

Engaging in missional ministry is not easy. Like Jesus, you may find yourself surrounded by a cloud of confusion. The church leaders were plotting; His devoted follower Mary was praising; the disciples were denying His death while debating their status; His close friend Judas was betraying Him, and all the while, Jesus celebrated the Passover and sang a hymn. Wouldn't it be wonderful if in spite of our trials we could celebrate and sing! Singing is such a powerful offering of praise to God that Jesus chose to end His Passover celebration with a song. Jesus was about to suffer the worse kind of capital punishment, yet His eyes were fixed on His mission and the heavenly prize.

If only we could be so singularly focused and mission minded with our offerings of praise. Our worship leadership would result in a message that ignites the minds and hearts of our members to become a missional church. Regardless of our circumstances, our songs would be a celebration of God's kingdom. But first let's define what a missional church is.

In the doctoral program at Andrews University Theological Seminary in Berrien Springs, Michigan, the missional church is defined in this way:

> A biblically formed 21st-century missionary movement of western culture. It defines the church as God's sent people. It is a way of life that models the incarnational life of Jesus Christ who took the form of His creation to show humankind the Father (John 14:9–11). Just as Christ transcended culture to show us the Father, the missional church transcends culture in order to show lost people Jesus Christ through sharing

life together. The result of the missional life is restoration of sinful people as we follow the ways of Christ through a deeper understanding of truth (John 14:6).[2]

Skip Bell, professor of Christian Leadership and director of the Doctor of Ministry Program at Andrews University adds, "A missional church is a local body of disciples who focus on a missionary understanding of God. God is missional; He enters the experience of His creation. Jesus is sent into the world to redeem. And missional churches today move in the everyday world as the presence of Jesus, incarnate in the world."[3]

CHRIST-CENTERED PRAISE

How can we have a missional ministry? How can we capture the incarnate presence of Jesus in our musical praise? Jesus' ministry model was relational and experiential. Jesus was sent. Jesus spent time with His disciples in order to train, mentor, and prepare them to experience the Father's love. With that purpose in mind, Jesus equipped and commissioned His disciples to go into the world to show His love to others. Our music ministry must be missional and Christ-centered. As we minister and relate to others, our music should be able to equip and commission our congregations. The worship experience must be filled with the transforming power of Jesus Christ. With our Christ-centered music, we are sent to save.

In order to accomplish this goal, we must understand the relational and experiential impact that music has on the listener. Eric Jensen, musician and author of the book, *Music with the Brain in Mind* admits, "Music may help activate the area in our brain most involved with mood, social skills, motivational development, cultural awareness, aesthetic appreciation, and self-discipline."[4] Music affects our emotional intelligence and impacts how we relate to people, places, and things around us. We cannot be like the chief priest, elders, and scribes who were willing to resort to trickery or gimmicks to appease the people. Our praise music and worship service must maintain its focus on Christ not the whims of our congregations. To maintain the focus on Jesus Christ our praise music should:

- Complement and support the worship message.

- Connect to the overall worship service theme.

- Prepare and soften hearts and minds for the sermon.

- Lead people to commit their lives to Jesus Christ.

Each aspect of the worship service should complement the sermon. You should work with your pastor to ensure that you have a weekly sermon synopsis and / or the theme of his or her message. This information is vital. When you have the theme for the sermon, then you can plan more intentionally. For example, if the theme for the day is redemption, then all aspects of the worship service (i.e., the praise songs, children's message, intercessory prayer, scripture readings, special music, etc.) should allude to or reference Christ's redemptive power. When this is done with purpose and planning, you create continuity. In this flow, the Holy Spirit will soften the hearts and minds of the people for the message. Structure does not hinder spontaneity. Planning does not hamper our praise. On the contrary, structure allows for spontaneity. Planning promotes praise. When you have a plan and you are properly prepared for the worship service, then you can relax and enjoy the free flowing of the Holy Spirit. Subsequently, when an altar call is made, people will be more inclined to surrender their hearts to God. By the power of the Holy Spirit, the Christ-centered worship service becomes a catalyst for conversion.

The worship leader is the person who manages the service flow, creates a cycle of praise, and gives people an opportunity to experience God. As worship leader, you should select songs that appeal to the hearts and minds of your congregation. You must be sensitive and use the worship segments to respond to the congregation's spiritual needs. The only way you can be aware of the spiritual needs of your congregation is if you are in touch with your pastor and in tune with the people. Like Christ, you must be one of the congregation. As a worship leader, you are most effective when you are part of the church's life. If you are just a visitor or a member who only comes to sing and then leaves, your ministry will lack deep relational and experiential power. If you hardly hear the sermon because you exit the church right after your worship set, how can you share the gospel? At best, your worship leading will have a fleeting emotional impact. People follow leaders that they know and trust. You may be worship leading, but the key question is: are people following?

You must strive to create a worship cycle that will take your congregation on a spiritual journey. You can intentionally transition your service segments and music from celebration (fast) to adoration (slow) for an atmosphere of meaningful worship that mirrors the ancient sanctuary service. This progression can happen once or multiple times in the service. However, it is this journey that creates a missional worship atmosphere that glorifies Jesus Christ. For praise to have a lasting impression, your congregation must experience a journey with Jesus. Here is how this worship cycle is accomplished at the traditional worship service held at the Sligo Seventh-day Adventist Church.

THE SLIGO CHURCH WORSHIP CYCLE

Prelude

Sligo Live!

Songs of Gathering

Welcome & Church Life

Hymn of Praise

Prayer

Anthem

Children's Message

Scripture

Music for Meditation

Sermon

Invitation to Give

Offertory

Hymn of Reflection

Benediction

Postlude

Sligo Worship Leader

- "The Worship Leader can take the people on a worship journey that mirrors the "Journey into the Holy of Holies" at every point. The leader must know where the people are and where he wants to take them and when they have arrived."

- Ps. 100 "Enter his gates with thanksgiving and into his courts with praise."

Barry Leisch, *The New Worship: Straight Talk on Music and the Church*

Worship Progression

- 5 Phases of Worship Progression (Ps. 100)

- Jubilation (Outer Court)   Celebration
                               ↓
- Thanksgiving (Gates)   Adoration

- Praise (Courts)

- Awe (Holy Place)

- Adoration (Most Holy Place)

Prelude

3 Praise Cycles Celebration	Sligo Live! Songs of Gathering Welcome & Church Life Hymn of Praise Prayer	Cycle #1
↓	Anthem Children's Message Scripture Music for Meditation **Sermon** **Invitation to Give**	Cycle #2
Adoration	Offertory **Hymn of Reflection** **Benediction**	Cycle #3

Postlude

At the Sligo Seventh-day Adventist Church where I serve as the pastor for worship, we have several service segments that create our worship cycle. Each segment (Prelude, Sligo Live!, Songs of Gathering, Welcome & Church Life, Hymn of Praise, Prayer, Anthem, Children's Message, Scripture, Music for Meditation, Sermon, Invitation to Give, Offertory, Hymn of Reflection, Benedicion, and Postlude) is outlined in the first box of the diagram on the previous page titled the *Sligo Worship Cycle.* In the second box titled *Sligo Worship Leader,* we give guidelines to our worship leaders. Our worship leaders are tasked to begin the worship journey. At Sligo, we follow a broader definition of worship leader. We use our pastors and elders to lead, manage, and coordinate the *entire* service, not just the musical elements. We believe that those leading out in worship must have a broader spiritual view of the service. Dr. Dean Kurtz agrees with this interpretation in his book *God's Word: The Final Word on Worship and Music.* He writes, "Worship leaders (by this I mean all those who stand before God's people and with their words or songs direct our thoughts toward God) are limited in their ability to effectively minister to the Lord and others if they lack a basic understanding of biblical principles governing worship and church music."[5] Accordingly, we have worship leaders for service coordination and choristers who lead out in singing.

Both our worship leaders and choristers are encouraged to:

- Focus comments on Christ, Scripture, or spiritual experiences.

- Prepare and practice transitions so they are smooth and seamless.

- Follow proper dress guidelines to minimize distractions (see Appendix III).

- Be theologically sound with lyrics or statements.

As worship leaders, we should refrain from persuading people to sing or participate. Our job is to profess the goodness and power of Jesus Christ. Our responsibility is to create an atmosphere that is spiritually inviting. Our role is to set a tone

> *Persuasion is the Holy Spirit's job.*

where the Holy Spirit can make the gospel of Jesus Christ irresistible to every worshiper. There is both an art and a science to salvation. In her book *Evangelism,* author Ellen White shares, "The science of salvation is to be the burden of every sermon, the theme of every song."[6] Famous Italian Renaissance painter, poet, artist, and sculptor Michelangelo explained the art of salvation saying, "True art is made noble and religious by the mind producing it. For those who feel it, nothing makes the soul so religious and pure as the endeavor to create something perfect, for God is perfection and whoever strives after it is striving after something divine."[7]

All service segments should be done with the art and science of worship in mind. We should strive for excellence and experience. If you employ proper planning, even your announcements can have a spiritual focus. Prepare your comments as well as your chord charts. Ensure that all service segments and transitions are Christ-centered, Scripture focused, deeply spiritual, and theologically sound. Clothing for praise teams should be coordinated. This may not apply to all worship settings, but when appropriate, this practice is useful. Uniformity tends to take the focus off individuals and place the focus on God. Therefore mentorship, preparation, and biblical training are vital for the worship leaders to take the congregation on a spiritual journey through the sanctuary as listed in the third box titled, *Worship Progression.*

Finally in the fourth box, I indicate that our worship service is comprised of *Three Praise Cycles* that flow from celebration to adoration. I like to say we have three praise cycles: one for the Father, one for the Son, and one for the Holy Spirit! All service segments serve to prepare and equip the people. Our aim is to create a seamless atmosphere of praise where the flow of the Holy

Spirit is experienced without distractions. As you look at our worship service, you will notice that Sligo has a few segments that may be uncommon. These segments are more common in a traditional style of worship. Some may even refer to our worship style as "high church." The majority of our music is played with the pipe organ and not by a pianist or praise band. So let me explain some of our segments. The *prelude* is the signal for a more focused response for worship to begin. It is the first movement of worship that creates a change in behavior and mindset. The prelude is our prompt to recognize and begin responding to the presence of God and the purposes of gathered worship. The purpose of the prelude is to enter into a holy space by quieting ourselves and preparing our hearts and minds.

Our first act of worship is gathering together. Simply by gathering, we are showing that God has worth. Where two or three are gathered in His name, Jesus Christ promises to be present (Matt. 18:20). Therefore, we sing the *songs of gathering.* In worship, we as a collective body gather in the presence of God. We are His invited guests who come before His throne. In our worship, we ask Christ to be present. Since we *ask* Him to be present, we should *expect* Him to be present. Therefore, we worship in expectation that the Holy Spirit will not only be in us but amongst us. When we gather to sing our songs, we are speaking words of praise and adulation to God.

God is the audience, and we
are His praise participants.

There is no other audience in worship but God!

Sligo Live! and our *Welcome and Church Life* are the ways in which we inform our members and online worshipers about ministry activities in the life of our church and community. We shoot live video each Sabbath on site. We produce a ten-minute live talk show with hosts and guests who inform our members about the events in our region. Then instead of announcements, we train our worship leaders to share about the ministry activities for the day and upcoming weeks in a way that also promotes the gospel of Jesus Christ. Our goal is to keep our focus on ministry and not just the management of our events. The *postlude* is the signal for sending the saints. It is the musical charge that sends us into this sinful world as ambassadors of Jesus Christ. When our worship is Christ-centered, we are empowered. No matter what type of church service, culture, or worship style you are accustomed to, Christ should be central. When we glorify Jesus Christ in our worship and keep Him central in our praise, then we are equipped to overcome the difficulties and trials the devil has devised.

CULTURAL PRAISE

Throughout His ministry, Jesus engaged in cultural praise. To seek and save the lost, Jesus' mission transcended race, culture, ethnicity, creed, social status, gender, politics, and religion. Anthropologist Edward Hall, author of the book *Beyond Culture,* explains the influence of culture. He writes, "Culture is man's medium; there is not one aspect of human life that is not touched and altered by culture. This means personality, how people express themselves (including shows of emotion), the way they think, how they move, how problems are solved, how their cities are planned and laid out, how transportation systems function and are organized, as well as how economic and government systems are put together and function."[8] Accordingly, Jesus exhibited supreme cultural intelligence. Dr. David Livermore, a thought leader in cultural intelligence and global leadership, states, "Cultural intelligence is the capability to function effectively across national, ethnic, and organizational cultures."[9] In His final hours, Jesus' sacrifice was cross-cultural.

As Jesus and His disciples left the Upper Room, a series of traumatic events ensued. First, Jesus predicted that all His disciples would leave Him and that Peter, His heir apparent, would deny

Him. Then He traveled with Peter, James, and John to the garden of Gethsemane to pray. This was one of the few times that Jesus prayed among His disciples instead of His customary private prayers. In this solemn and sacred moment, Jesus was in desperate need of deliverance (Matt. 26:39). Yet His friends were sleeping. The chief priest and elders sent a mob with swords and clubs to the garden to capture Christ. Then Jesus was arrested after Judas identified Him with a treasonous kiss. During Jesus' arrest, Peter tried to fight to free Him. But instead, he wounded the servant of the high priest by cutting off his ear (John 18:10; Luke 22:50). Then Jesus performed His last miracle before His crucifixion: "And He touched his ear and healed him" (Luke 22:51). "Then all the disciples forsook Him and fled" (Matt. 26:56).

I believe it is significant that before Jesus was crucified, He performed His last miracle on the high priest's servant. It is very likely this servant was a Levite since the Levites served the priests (Num. 3:6). It is also significant that Jesus' final miracle was to restore the Levite's hearing. As we noted before, hearing in Hebrew culture is considered the seat of wisdom and intelligence. Although the Levites were among the most educated leaders in Israel, they were deaf and dumb to their Deliverer. They misunderstood and rejected Christ's message. The Levites and priests who were called to promote the gospel of Jesus Christ were unmoved by its promises (Mal. 2:7). Because they were stubborn, they could not hear Christ's call. Sadly, they were unable to comprehend the magnitude of their sin.

Are we like this Levite? Are we living in the final hours of Jesus Christ's ministry to the world so preoccupied with our own traditions and music methods that we have missed His mission? Are we like the angry mob standing in the midst of the garden of God's love, yet refusing to hear what the Spirit is saying? Jesus restored the Levite's hearing as an eternal example that He would forgive any sinner if they would only listen and obey His words. Let's not be as the Levite who was deaf to Christ's call. Let's open our ears and hearts so we can hear Christ's voice (Heb. 3:15).

That night, Jesus was taken to Caiaphas at the Sanhedrin to stand trial. There Jesus was tried and convicted. During the trial, Jesus was lied to, spat upon, and beaten (Matt. 26:60–61, 67). Then, to make matters worse, Peter denied Him. In the morning Jesus' final hearing took place before the Roman governor Pontius Pilate. When Judas heard that Christ had been convicted, he committed suicide (Matt. 27:5). Now, one of Jesus' own disciples and close friend was lost to sin. At the palace, Pilate asked Jesus if He was indeed the King of the Jews. Jesus responded with a five word answer that was overflowing with his love and grace for Pilate. "He answered and said to him, 'It is as you say'" (Mark 15:2). And then, like the good preacher, Jesus remained silent. His plan was to speak directly to Pilate's conscience and give him an opportunity to repent.

There are times in our ministries when we need to keep silent. When you are being falsely accused, let your sanctified silence speak. Let your silence send a message of God's love, favor, and protection. You don't always have to respond to criticisms, rumors, and accusations. Jesus Christ used silence as a teacher and a testimony. Silence speaks volumes! It was Jesus' moment of silence that caused Pilate to marvel (Mark 15:5). Let Christ's example of silence be a lesson to us today. We must be like Jesus and learn when it is time to silently teach instead of preach. Several times, it seemed like Pilate heard the Holy Spirit's voice. In response, he made repeated efforts to substitute Barabbas for Jesus: "So when they had gathered, Pilate said to them, 'Whom do you want me to release to you: Barabbas, or Jesus who is called the Christ?' For he knew that it was out of envy that they had delivered him up" (Matt. 27:17–18, ESV).

While Pilate was sitting on the judgment seat, his wife came to him and pleaded for Jesus' release. God had given her a dream that disturbed her soul. She knew Christ was a just and innocent man. But the church leaders had already persuaded the multitude to crucify Jesus. So Pilate rephrased his question:

> The governor again said to them, "Which of the two do you want me to release for you?" And they said, "Barabbas." Pilate said to them, "Then what shall I do with Jesus who is called Christ?" They all said, "Let him be crucified!" And he said, "Why, what evil has he done?" But they shouted all the more, "Let him be crucified!" So when Pilate saw that he was gaining nothing, but rather that a riot was beginning, he took water and washed his hands before the crowd, saying, "I am innocent of this man's blood; see to it yourselves."
>
> —MATTHEW 27:21–24, ESV

Three times Pilate presented Jesus to the people as innocent. Three times, the Holy Spirit entered his conscience and urged him to do what was right. But the people refused. So Pilate may have washed his hands of the crime. But he could not cleanse his soul. He refused to surrender his political pride and thereby ordered Christ's execution. Instead of looking deeper or being praised throughout the centuries for his humility, Pilate arguably ordered the greatest crime in history: "Then he released Barabbas to them; and when he had scourged Jesus, he delivered Him to be crucified" (Matt. 27:26). A group of soldiers striped, tortured, mocked, ridiculed, beat, spat on, and even pretended to worship Jesus (Mark 15:19). They led Him away to Golgotha weakened and bloodied. They nailed Him to the cross and crucified Him between two thieves. Even in His disgrace and shame, Jesus was central. He had become a sovereign spectacle for all the world to see. Jesus came to be lifted up and crucified on the cross. His disciples deserted Him, yet many women who had been His followers and ministered to Him stood looking from a distance (Matt. 27:55–56).

Jesus bore the weight of sin and the physical, mental, and spiritual pain of suffering for all humankind. His agony was unbearable. Yet He worshiped! His pain was intolerable. Yet He praised! Jesus uttered a song of suffering and praise on the cross: "And about the ninth hour Jesus cried out with a loud voice, saying, '*Eli, Eli lama sabachthani?'* that is, '*My God, My God, why have You forsaken Me?*'" (Matt. 27:46). In His suffering, Jesus sang! He cried out the lyrics of David's Psalm 22 and spoke to God the Father in a Messianic melody. In her blog comment posted in *Christianity Today,* Amy Becker explains, "For Jewish people like Jesus, who knew the Hebrew Scriptures and who used the Psalms as a songbook, the opening line of any psalm served as a reference to the whole. 'My God, My God, why have You forsaken Me?' is the opening line of Psalm 22. Similarly, when Jesus cries out using the initial line of Psalm 22, He is referring His listeners to the entirety of the psalm."[10]

Jesus knew that in His moment of separation and abject despair, God would inhabit His praise (Ps. 22:3). Although the lyrics of Psalm 22 begin in tribulation for one man, they end in global triumph for all men:

> All the ends of the world
> > Shall remember and turn to the LORD,
> And all the families of the nations
> > Shall worship before You.
> For the Kingdom is the LORD'S
> > And He rules over the nations.
> All the prosperous of the earth
> > Shall eat and worship;
> All those who go down to the dust
> > Shall bow before Him,
> Even he who cannot keep himself alive.
>
> —PSALM 22:27–29

In His final moments, Jesus remained true to His mission. At the Cross, He took the time to seek and save the lost. Jesus' mission created a Christ-centered culture. His lifestyle of praise preempted position, politics, gender, ethnicity, tradition, and religious practice. Jesus was surrounded by various people and cultures. He called a diverse group of Jews (fishermen, a tax collector, a zealot, and a

Canaanite) to be His disciples. He offered Judas (His betrayer) a chance to repent when He predicted his betrayal. He performed a miracle and reattached the Levite's ear in an attempt to demonstrate His love for the religious leaders. He offered grace to Roman governor Pontus Pilate, indicating that there is room at the Cross for oppressors and politicians. While on the cross, He interceded in prayer for His executioners to show His care for the salvation of the Gentiles (Luke 23:34). Jesus showed no gender bias. Several women followed close behind Him and were with Him when He died (Luke 23:49).

Jesus' conviction and commission to offer the plan of salvation was cross-cultural. Dr. Pedrito Maynard-Reid, theologian and contributor to the *Complete Library of Christian Worship* states in his book, *Diverse Worship,*

> Culture therefore goes beyond language, dialect and speech. It includes everything that is passed on, experienced, and practiced. It involves information, education, techniques, and inventions. It comprises customs, habits, aesthetic choices, beliefs rites, traditions, myths, legends, superstitions, stories, songs, dances, jokes, tastes, inherited artifacts, prejudices, attitudes, and values—in short, everything that is part of one's social heritage and environment.[11]

Therefore, it is not just our musical style that creates cross-cultural worship. During his lecture at the 2015 NEC Ministerial Music Conference, musician and songwriter Nicholas Zork contended that "cross-cultural worship is only possible within the culture of the Cross."[12] A. W. Tozer, regarded as one of the deepest theological thinkers of the twentieth century further states, "Worship is no longer worship when it reflects the culture around us more than the Christ within us."[13]

The Cross of Christ is the culture of our worship.

For the Christian, the Cross of Christ supersedes culture and transcends time. As Christians, the Cross of Christ recreates our culture. It determines our personalities, emotions, thoughts, movements, problem-solving techniques, personal and family plans, economics, government systems, communities, and more. The Cross of Christ with its redemption power is our heritage. Jesus' path to the Cross was the ultimate worship journey. Jesus Christ made Himself a spectacle so that we could be spiritual.

As we design worship services for our congregations, we are captured, even arrested, by culture. Many of us believe that in order to worship, we must have an experience that reflects our own cultures. We divide ourselves in an effort to create cultural worship services (young vs. old, African-American vs. Caucasian, European vs. American, Asian vs. Hispanic)—and the list goes on. We focus our worship styles solely on the heritage of our birth (European, African, African-American, Hispanic, Caribbean, Middle-Eastern, Asian, etc.). We segregate ourselves "righteously" so we can maintain our worship rituals. We congregate by cultures and sanction this practice because we will not sacrifice our style of praise. While our expressions of praise may be diverse, it is Christ alone who unifies. While our styles of worship may satisfy, it is Christ alone who sanctifies. Our musical heritage does not make us holy. Let me be clear: there is nothing wrong with cultural music and diverse worship styles. Culture is a vital part of our humanity, and variety reflects God's divinity. However, when our quest for culture supersedes our Christianity, then we are on dangerous, shallow ground! If we are not Christ-centered, even our diversity may become our downfall.

On the Cross, Christ was elevated high above anyone or anything else. All eyes were fixed on Him as the central figure. Despite all the cultures that were represented, the Cross of Christ was preeminent. Oh, if we could do that today with our worship styles! There would be joy in heaven if our focus could be on the Cross as our culture and not on the culture we bring to the Cross. If Jesus became the central focus of our worship, then our cultural heritage would be

Christ first and everything else second. Then we would celebrate our differences and not seek to diminish the beauty of our diversity. We would not complain when the music isn't from our culture because our focus would be on the culture of the Cross! In that moment, we would be silent and let the process of sanctification satisfy, instead of our preoccupation with style. As a family of Christians, we would be tolerant of each other's musical heritage and not consider diversity heresy. Christ's love would fill our hearts and minds so that our goal would be heaven—our true eternal heritage.

What can we do in our worship services to create a Christ-centered culture? I must admit I don't know all the answers to that question. I believe through prayer and Bible study God will continue to reveal His plan to His people. However, here are some tips to begin your worship journey to the Cross where Christ is exalted:

- **Cultivate blended worship**: Use diverse musical genres to help bridge generational and cultural gaps. Sing worship music that inspires the people in *your* church.

- **Sanction corporate singing**: Refrain from giving a concert. Prepare worship sets that allow people to sing the songs they know and enjoy. Allow the Holy Spirit to move among *all* the people in your congregation.

- **Properly interpret praise responses**: Do not be quick to judge the merits of conservative or liberal responses to praise. Remember, *only* the Holy Spirit truly knows hearts and reads minds.

- **Create melodic consistency**: Create consistent melodies to support the service that reflect the gospel of Jesus Christ.

- **Present songs properly**: Be intentional when introducing new songs and concepts. Only teach one new song per worship set. Be patient and let the congregation learn the music. Make changes methodically.

- **Offer Christ your best:** Always offer your absolute best to Christ in order to please God with your sacrifice of praise.

ETERNAL PRAISE

I began serving as the volunteer minister of music at CPC on August 5, 2000. Three months later, the Lord intervened in my corporate career, and suddenly I found myself unemployed. The reason behind my job loss was extremely peculiar. I was a successful executive director in healthcare marketing. I supervised a statewide sales team that far exceeded their monthly and annual quotas. Yet a seemingly simple misunderstanding left me unemployed. I left my thirteen-year corporate career perplexed, knowing that my abrupt termination was God's divine intervention. So I focused on ministry. After several months of serving solely as the minister of music, I felt inadequate. Although I had years of musical experience, I felt unprepared to be the *minister* of music. I prayed for spiritual guidance and began my search for ministry knowledge. I read about a worship leadership course advertised in *Worship Leader Magazine*. So I made a request to my pastor to take this week-long, non-degree course offered at Regent University in Virginia Beach, Virginia. It was during this course that the Lord clearly spoke to me again and again. At the end of the week, and after many unmistakable, God-inspired moments, my heart was full and my mind made up. I would pursue a graduate degree in worship.

While I served at the CPC, I applied to Regent University's School of Divinity. I was accepted into the program in August 2001 and began a full-time pursuit of a Master of Arts degree in Practical Theology, Worship, and Renewal. Now with only one income and a young child, my husband and I were devastated financially. As you can imagine, these were very lean, dry years. Yet spiritually we were rich, full, and drinking from a deep well of God's love and blessings. During this dry spell, God made a promise to me. He told me that He would "redeem the time" (Eph. 5:16–17). I was not sure what that meant; however, I believed it. I claimed His promise daily.

Our financial situation worsened as we struggled to pay my tuition. Although the Lord blessed me with 90 percent of my tuition paid in scholarships and grants, the remaining 10 percent was still difficult to muster. Yet we did not despair. Instead, we became living witnesses of Psalm 37:25, "I have been young, and now am old; yet I have not seen the righteous forsaken, nor his descendants begging bread." We knew that ministry was God's plan for me, and by faith we would succeed. Miracle after miracle happened to sustain and strengthen us. Then by God's grace in May 2004, I graduated with my Master of Arts degree in Practical Theology, Worship, and Renewal. In January 2005, I became a part-time, conference-paid employee at CPC. My small income was a big help in our home. God would repay our sacrifice.

Then God spoke to me again through His Word (Isa. 61:6) and by placing godly people in my path. During a breakfast symposium for the graduates, I conversed with our keynote speaker Rear Admiral Barry C. Black, 62nd Chaplain of the U.S. Senate. He advised me to get a doctorate in Strategic Leadership. He said, "Our church needs highly qualified leaders who understand biblical worship practice." So I did. I enrolled in the doctorate program. My emphasis was worship leadership. Four years later, in May 2008, I graduated with my doctorate in Strategic Leadership from Regent University. So after five years as a volunteer, eight years as the part-time, employed minister of music (that included seven years of post-graduate studies), on October 1, 2013, I was hired to full-time pastoral ministry at the Sligo SDA Church, the largest Seventh-Day Adventist church in our region.

God's promises are true. He redeemed the time. I spent thirteen years in corporate America and thirteen years preparing for full-time ministry. I am passionate about pastoring. For this, I give all glory, honor, and eternal praise to God! My personal mission statement is "to be a vessel through which God creates a sea of worshipers." My personal vision statement is "leading worship for eternity." I know these *Deeper Praise* principles have enriched my life and furthered my mission. My worship journey has not been easy, but my path to God's praise is packed with His promises. I continue to go deeper. Now every day, I am saturated by God's majesty and love.

You too, can begin your worship journey. Your path to deeper praise is promised once you become a Christ-centered Levite who studies God's Word. May God keep you faithful as you journey on your eternal path to deeper praise.

> Blessed be the LORD God, the God of Israel, who only does wondrous things! And blessed be His glorious name forever! And let the whole earth be filled with His glory. Amen and Amen.
>
> —PSALM 72:18–20

LEVITE LESSONS

1. Without mission, our music lacks depth, produces mayhem, and will weaken our connection to Jesus Christ.

2. As musicians, we must give our priorities, dreams, and hopes to God.

3. Our praise must have the ability to penetrate beyond the walls of the church in order to change the world.

4. With our Christ-centered music, we are sent to save.

5. By the power of the Holy Spirit, the Christ-centered worship service becomes a catalyst for conversion.

6. The only way you can be aware of the spiritual needs of your congregation is if you are in touch with your pastor and in tune with the people.

7. For praise to have a lasting impression, your congregation must experience a journey with Jesus.

8. The Cross of Christ is the culture of our worship.

PRACTICAL PRAISE QUESTIONS

Who else do you know who could benefit from taking this *Deeper Praise* journey?

How can you actively share your newfound *Deeper Praise* ministry path with others?

ENDNOTES

1.   Joseph Scriven, "What a Friend We Have in Jesus," quoted in Robert J. Morgan, *Then Sings My Soul: 150 of the World's Greatest Hymn Stories* (Nashville, TN: Thomas Nelson, 2003), 130.

2.   Andrews University (Berrien Springs, MI), 2015, https://www.andrews.edu/sem/dmin/concentrations/missional_church/, accessed on May 17, 2015.

3.   Skip Bell, DMin. "What is a Missional Church," E-News Letter, Sligo SDA Church (Takoma Park, MD), 2015, http://sligochurch.org/what-is-a-missional-church/, accessed on May 17, 2015.

4.   Eric Jensen, *Music with the Brain in Mind* (Thousand Oaks, CA: Cowin Press, 2000), 45.

5.   Dean Kurtz, *God's Word, The Final Word on Worship and Music: A Biblical Study* (Maitland, FL: Xulon Press, 2008), 6.

6.   Ellen G. White, *Evangelism* (Washington: Review and Herald Publishing Assoc., 1946), 502.

7.   Sarah Knowles Bolton, *Famous European Artists* (New York: Thomas Crowell & Co., 1890). 55.

8.   Edward T. Hall, *Beyond Culture* (New York: Anchor Books 1989), 16.

9.   David Livermore, *Leading with Cultural Intelligence: The New Secret to Success* (New York: American Management Association, 2010), 4.

10.   Amy Julia Becker, "The Song Jesus Sang on the Cross," *Thin Places, A Blog by Amy Julia Becker,* April 17, 2004, http://www.christianitytoday

.com/amyjuliabecker/2014/april/song-jesus-sang-on-cross.html, accessed on June 7, 2015.

11.   Pedrito Maynard-Reid, *Diverse Worship: African-American, Caribbean & Hispanic Perspectives* (Downers Grove, IL: Inter Varsity Press, 2000), 18.

12.   Nicholas Zork, lecture, "Cross Cultural Worship: A Biblical Vision of Embodied Practice," NEC Ministerial Music Conference, New Jerusalem Baptist Church, Rochdale Village, NY, April 17–18, 2015.

13.   A. W. Tozer, https://mobile.twitter.com/tozeraw/status/61012882612 7904768, accessed on October 5, 2015.

Appendix I

THE LEVITE PRAISE PLEDGE

He appointed some of the Levites to minister before the ark of the Lord, to make petition, to give thanks, and to praise the LORD, the God of Israel.

—1 CHRONICLES 16:4, NIV

*D*EAR LEVITE:

Thank you for your decision to offer God your talents and time in ministry service. As a spiritual Levite, you now pledge to honor God by giving Him your first and best fruits as a sacrifice of praise. This means you will devote yourself as a humble servant leader to discipling others through the ministry of worship. You pledge to use your talents in music, the arts, and all areas of praise and worship to glorify God alone, not yourself or others.

Here are some of the characteristics of a spiritual Levite:

- A Levite is a worshiper who pleases God with his praise.

- A Levite devotes herself to Bible study to deepen her relationship with Jesus Christ.

- A Levite is called of God and uses his talents to glorify God.

- A Levite is a consecrated servant leader and consummate learner.

- A Levite is grateful for constructive feedback in order to give God her best.

- A Levite is committed to his team's spiritual growth and well-being.

- A Levite desires God's acceptance more than human accolades.

- A Levite understands that consecration is essential for dedication.

- A Levite comes to worship prepared and in a spirit of praise.

- A Levite practices so that she has the freedom to experience God in worship.

- A Levite is led by the Holy Spirit so that each song becomes a sermon.

- A Levite uses his pastoral responsibility to lead and guide others in love.

I, (print name) _____ have decided to devote myself to God as a spiritual Levite. I have searched my heart and believe that God has called me to commit my time and talents to Him through music ministry. I will give God my best efforts and serve Him, by His grace, to the best of my ability.

_____

Signature   **Date**

Appendix II

THE MEANING OF MUSIC:
CLASSROOM EXERCISE

*I*N A COURSE I teach at Washington Adventist University called "Christian Worship and Church Music," I give the class an exercise on the meaning of music. Based on their musical preferences, I select four songs that I believe will be unfamiliar to most of the students. I select an equal mix of instrumental and vocal music.

I played the following four songs:

- "The Wandering Kind," by Josh Groban
- "A Partial History of Black Music, Handel's Soulful Messiah," by Mervyn Warren (Instrumental)
- "I Won't Let Go," by Rascal Flatts
- "Redemption," by Michael W. Smith (Instrumental)

Then I asked each student to answer the following questions or statements for each song:

1. Is this song sacred or secular?

2. List three words you would use to describe this tune.

3. What emotions do you feel?

4. State in one sentence the message the music is sending.

5. What would you title this song?

The results of this exercise were powerful. With little to no knowledge of the songs, students were able to determine the core meaning of the music just by listening. Let's look at their combined answers to each song on the following pages.

SONG #1: "THE WANDERING KIND," BY JOSH GROBAN (SECULAR)

1. Is this song sacred or secular?
   Answer: 89 percent answered "secular."

2. List three words you would use to describe this tune.
   Answer: Celtic, folksy, energetic, quaint, pleasant, playful, adventurous, joyous, happy, lively, determined, Irish, varied modality, movie soundtrack, countryside, journey, magical, peaceful.

3. What emotions do you feel?
   Answer: Freedom, noble, passionate, courageous, peaceful, calm, relaxing, lighthearted, jovial, indifferent, comfortable, happy, joyous, hope.

4. State in one sentence the message the music is sending.
   This song is sending a message of freedom, expectation, of something new that is coming.
   The journey will have its ups and downs, but you will prevail.
   Enjoy life and live.
   Life is an adventure.
   Be happy and enjoy your life.
   Go do something adventurous.
   Victory song
   Happy moments will come no matter how ugly it may look.

5. What would you title this song?
   Answer: "An Open Road," "Heading out on a Journey," "The Irish Man," "Spring Time," "Glorious Name," "The Departure," "An Adventure."

SONG #2: "A PARTIAL HISTORY OF BLACK MUSIC, HANDEL'S SOULFUL MESSIAH," BY MERVYN WARREN (SACRED MUSIC HIGHLIGHTING SECULAR MUSIC STYLE THROUGH THE DECADES)

1. Is this song sacred or secular?

   Answer: 55 percent answered "secular"; 45 percent answered "sacred."

2. List three words you would use to describe this tune.

   Answer: Percussive, rhythmic, diverse, joyous, tribal, jazzy, pop, churchy, hurried, anxious, woeful, joy, freedom, peace, creepy, mystery, random, spontaneous, expressive, entertainment, African culture, Gospel, anger, possession, romantic, night, party, guilt, power.

3. What emotions do you feel?

   Answer: Anger, sadness, tragic event, boxing, dancing, fighting, joyous, tribulation, fierce, aggressive, confused, uneasy, distrust, anxiety, sympathy, worry, encouraged, happy, relaxed, expectant, fear, excitement, interest.

4. State in one sentence the message the music is sending.

   This song sends a message about the diversity of music in the African-American community.

   The struggle.

   The dangerous traps that lay ahead.

   The plight from slavery to freedom.

   The movement of a people.

   There are different stages and emotions in life.

5. A tragic sense of someone going through a depressing and dramatic life. What would you title this song?

Answer: "Wildlife," "Music Remix," "Bipolar Habitation," "The Chase for Freedom," "The Random Praise Remix," "Movement of a People," "Messiah's Mix," "Facing the Amazon," "Panorama."

SONG #3: "I WON'T LET GO," BY RASCAL FLATTS (SECULAR)

1. Is this song sacred or secular?
   Answer: 90 percent answered "secular."

2. List three words you would use to describe this tune.
   Answer: Emotive, building, comfortable, inspirational, heartfelt, emotional, contemplative, encouraged, love, calm, motivation, peaceful, romantic, soothing, trust, commitment, friend, family, sadness, lonely, careless.

3. What emotions do you feel?
   Answer: Sadness, disappointed, dependency, joy, encouraged, safe, hope, lonely, reflective, pensive, unsure, love, contemplative, strengthened, peaceful, tearful.

4. State in one sentence the message the music is sending.
   No one is alone.
   Someone to hold on to.
   I'll stand with you through life's troubles.
   This song conveys love and support for someone.
   Don't give up on love in the hard times.
   A love song for couples.
   There will always be someone who will help me.
   You are not alone; there is someone to support you.
   Offers to help in tough moments.

5. What would you title this song?

Answer: "Stand by You," "I Will Stand by You," "Someone to Hold on to," "I Will," "Love in Tough Moments," "I Will Always Hold You."

(Note: The composer is a Christian.)

SONG #4: "REDEMPTION," BY MICHAEL W. SMITH (SACRED / CLASSICAL)

1. Is this song sacred or secular?

Answer: 60 percent answered "sacred"; 40 percent answered "secular."

2. List three words you would use to describe this tune.

Answer: Playful, animated, frustrated, children, playing, moving, joy, tears, romantic, hope, happy, cartoons, building, back and forth, melodious, contemplative, harmonious, peaceful, calm, attractive, aspiring, majestic, worshipful.

3. What emotions do you feel?

Answer: Excited, passionate, celebration, determined, striving, desiring, happy, majestic, intrigued, at ease, joyful, hopeful, surprised, heavenly, peaceful.

4. State in one sentence the message the music is sending.

The song has a message to reflect on one's life.
Discussions are over; let's go home.
This is a song of hope.
There is hope, and we can rejoice in it now.
Celebrate creation.
We will always have to start from the bottom.

5. What would you title this song?
   Answer: "A New Start," "Dawn of Creation,"
   "Journey," "A New Day," "Hymn Tune Variations,"
   "Christmas Is Here," "Home," "A Life's Journey," "At
   the End of the Tunnel."

(Note: The composer modeled this music after famous movie scores.)

Appendix III

SLIGO CHURCH DRESS GUIDELINES*

*A*LL ATTIRE FOR males and females should be modest and appropriate for entering the sanctuary and for leading out in worship. Clothing should not be a distraction to the congregation. If jewelry is worn, it must be modest. Even in more relaxed events, such as concerts, be mindful that you are participating in leading worship. Therefore, dress appropriately!

RULES FOR ALL PARTICIPANTS

(Male and female apply where appropriate):

1. Be modest and tasteful in your attire.

2. Be mindful that you are entering God's house. Please act and dress accordingly.

3. Skirts should be no shorter than knee length both when standing and sitting down on the platform.

4. No spaghetti-strap, thin strap, or strapless tops should be worn.

5. No low-cut necklines on dresses or blouses.

6. Do not wear tight clothing while ministering.

7. Be mindful that you are above the congregation. Clothing that looks appropriate in your mirror at

---

* These guidelines suit the diverse demographics of the Sligo SDA church. For various congregations, other guidelines may or may not apply.

home will look shorter when you are at a higher angle.

8. Please wear makeup modestly.

9. Formal or business casual church attire is appropriate.

Make sure that clothing never makes *you* the focus of worship. God must always be the focus of our praise.

BIBLIOGRAPHY

Bolton, Sarah Knowles. *Famous European Artists*. New York: Thomas Cromwell & Co., 1890.

Brand, Chad, Draper, Charles, and England, Archie. *Holman Illustrated Bible Dictionary*. Nashville, TN: Holman Bible Publishers, 2003.

Curtis, Edward M. *Ancient Psalms and Modern Worship*. Evangelical Theological Society Papers, 1992.

Doukhan, Jacques B. *Proverbs*. Nampa, ID: Pacific Press Publishing, 2014.

Doukhan, Lilliane. *In Tune with God*. Hagerstown, MD: Autumn House Pub., 2009.

Futato, Mark, and Howard Jr., David M. *Interpreting the Psalms*. Grand Rapids, MI: Kregel Pub., 2007.

Greenleaf, Robert K. *The Servant-Leader Within*. New York: Paulist Press, 2003.

Hall, Edward T. *Beyond Culture*. New York: Anchor Books, 1989.

Hunter, James C. *The World's Most Powerful Leadership Principle*. NY: Crown Business, 2004.

Jensen, Eric. *Music with the Brain in Mind*. Thousand Oaks, CA: Corwin Press, 2000.

Johansson, Calvin M. *Music & Ministry: A Biblical Counterpoint, 2nd ed*. Peabody, MA: Hendrickson Pub., 1998.

Juslin, Patrik N., and Sloboda, John A. *Music and Emotion: Theory and Research.* New York, Oxford: Oxford UP, 2001.

Kurtz, Dean. *God's Word: The Final Word on Worship and Music.* Maitland, FL: Xulon Press, 2008.

Liesch, Barry W. *The New Worship: Straight Talk on Music and the Church.* Grand Rapids, MI: Baker Books, 2001.

Livermore, David. *Leading with Cultural Intelligence.* New York: American Management Assoc., 2010.

Maynard-Reid, Pedrito U. *Diverse Worship.* Downers Grove, IL: InterVarsity Press, 2000.

Miller, Patrick D. *Interpreting the Psalms.* Philadelphia: Fortress Press, 1986.

Morgan, Robert J. *Then Sings My Soul.* Nashville, TN: Thomas Nelson, 2003.

Piper, John. *Taste and See.* Sisters, OR: Multnomah, 2005.

Radmacher, Earl D. *The Nelson Study Bible.* Nashville, TN: Thomas Nelson, 1997.

Sorge, Bob. *Exploring Worship.* Lee's Summit, MO: Oasis House, 2001.

Vine, W. E., Unger, Merrill F., and White, William. *Vine's Complete Expository Dictionary of Old and New Testament Words.* Nashville, TN: Thomas Nelson, 1996.

Walton, John H, Matthews, Victor H., and Chavalas, Mark W. *The IVP Bible Background Commentary: Old Testament.* Downers Grove, IL: InterVarsity Press, 2000.

White, Ellen G., *Evangelism.* Washington: Review and Herald Pub., 1946.

_____. *Patriarchs and Prophets.* Mountain View, CA: Pacific Press, 1958.

_____. *Steps to Christ.* Mountain View, CA: Pacific Press, 1948.

_____. *Testimonies for the Church.* Mountain View, CA: Pacific Press, 1948.

Young, Sarah. *Jesus Today.* Nashville, TN: Thomas Nelson, 2012.

Zinke, Rosalie. *Worship.* Nampa, ID: Pacific Press, 2011.

ABOUT THE AUTHOR

DR. CHERYL WILSON-BRIDGES is the pastor for worship at the Sligo Seventh-Day Adventist Church in Takoma Park, Maryland, as well as an adjunct professor of Christian worship and church music at Washington Adventist University. A talented presenter, accomplished group singer, and worship leader, she is also the author of *Levite Praise: God's Biblical Design for Praise and Worship* (Creation House).

Dr. Bridges holds a master's degree in Practical Theology (Worship and Renewal) and a doctorate in Strategic Leadership from Regent University. She resides in Upper Marlboro, Maryland, with her husband, Conrad, and son, Darius, who are essential components of her life and ministry.

CONTACT THE AUTHOR

*D*R. CHERYL WILSON-BRIDGES speaks frequently on the topic of praise and worship leadership. For more information, purchase your copy of *Levite Praise: God's Biblical Design for Praise and Worship.*

To schedule a worship seminar, please send an email to: levitepraise3@gmail.com.